LEFT OUT IN AMERICA

THE STATE OF HOMELESSNESS IN THE UNITED STATES

Pat LaMarche

CHARLES BRUCE FOUNDATION
CARLISLE, PA

Originally Published By
Upala Press 2006
Portland, Maine 04102
www.upalapress.com

Book design & cover photos: Chad Bruce
Printed and bound in the United States

DEDICATION

For Becky and John, the reasons
I love going home

And, for Carl. who taught me
that the whole world is my home.

CONTENTS

FORWARD

Rarely, if ever, has a candidate for Vice President of the United States stepped through the doors of a homeless shelter for more than a spurious photo op, a la Paul Ryan's stint sloshing soapsuds in the Ohio soup kitchen during his failed 2012 campaign. For sure, none have slept in shelters and on the streets, spent time hanging with folks without homes, championed their cause, or written a compelling, insightful book about her 2-week tour of shelters across America. *Left Out In America: The State of Homelessness In the United States* reflects the unconventional campaign expedition of Pat LaMarche, Green Party Vice President candidate in the 2004 election.

Homelessness—as it affects upward of 10 million mostly invisible babies, toddlers, children, teens, young adults, women and men—reflects a serious gap and gross neglect in this, the wealthiest country in the history of the world. *Left Out In America* explores behind-the-scenes and illuminates human heartbreak of this social issue that seems to have defied mainstream political will or solutions, case in point, the underfunded, under-focused and underperforming federal 10 Year Plan to End Homelessness.

Left out of self-serving political considerations, left out of earnest media coverage, and left out of mainstream community support, people experiencing homelessness are discarded like yesterday's garbage, reliant on too little charity and good will, kept alive by unheralded kindness from their community on the streets and a few caring souls who refuse to ignore the human tragedy of houseless kids and adults found in virtually every community.

Pat astutely realized her chances for success as Green Party Vice Presidential nominee, despite the integrity and intelligence she and her ticket-mate David Cobb brought to the campaign, were as slim as the possibility of nuclear power plants being replaced by clean energy. But she flung herself into the media opportunity this unfeasible crusade offered, and lined up a 14-day tour of homeless shelters. Her childhood in Providence, RI public housing projects and her innate sensitivity to the downtrodden failed to protect her from the brutal realities of life without a home on this tour. Her comfort level, a modest standard compared to most, was quickly and repeatedly shattered. But she persisted.

Her once-in-a-lifetime itinerary bounced coast to coast, finding no shortage of forgotten and abandoned souls willing to sit down and share their experiences of hardships and their hopes for the future. "Lady Vice President" slept in shelters next to coughing babies, was rousted by police as she and her bedraggled entourage made their presence known on the streets, and witnessed the violence that erupts when people feel left out.

Imagine one of the "left out" women getting to actually dialogue with a candidate for vice president. Many spoke; Pat listened, and promised to relate their stories. *Left Out In America* poignantly reflects the hard times besetting those who did their best to pursue the American Dream but ended up with the American Nightmare.

Pat heard from red-blooded Americans, including veterans, whose lives were upended by poverty, domestic violence, family dysfunction, job loss, illness, and a host of other combinations that hard luck throws at the unwary and debilitated. Their stories fill this insightful book, sagas that wouldn't be told elsewhere, chronicled by a woman with a commitment to making things right for those left out.

Pat's trek does not bypass the tender kindnesses and head-shaking humor for those sensitive enough to notice. Avoiding stereotypes of most media outlets, Pat reveals the humans behind the leprosy-like label "the homeless." Sad and funny tales, heartwarming and heartbreaking anecdotes unveil indiscriminate human condition and human frailty, bureaucratic insanity and deteriorated mental stability.

Homelessness—under-reported and inadequately addressed—reflects widespread poverty, economic injustice and long-term neglect of low income populations as well as plundering the vulnerable by Wall Street robber barons and unscrupulous bankers. A candid and talented journalist, LaMarche points to carnage, leaving no doubt that, despite human frailty that may contribute to the tumble to the streets, systemic failures upend whatever tenuous terrain these hapless feet used to stand on. Amidst chaos endemic to the shredded safety net, an alien environment to most Americans, LaMarche adeptly leaves intact the dignity and beauty of those who surround her on this staggering campaign trip.

LaMarche's penchant for an underdog fight provides her with plenty of motivation to weave stories of hardship and hope into evidence of economic and systemic injustice. From a lifetime of involvement with those left out, this political maven and media-savvy mother packed her backpack, grabbed her sleeping bag and stalwartly set out to chronicle stories from the streets of Maine to California.

Pat LaMarche is no ordinary politician. She's more of an investment specialist. She's put her values on the table and double-dog-dares the rest of America, including Ivory Tower leaders, to contribute to the restoration of the fast-growing segment of kids and adults who've been left out. Her political savvy and her Irish wit combine with her plain spoken, common sense observations about this broken infrastructure that shatters lives and shreds futures.

She leaves readers with solid reasons why homelessness is more than a failure of society to care for those who stumble. Her stories amply illustrate the fall-out from "haves" pattern of inequity and iniquity that leads to a crumbling of life's dreams and basic refuge for millions of "have nots," left out children, youth and adults, our brothers and sisters, sons and daughters, nieces and nephews, neighbors and co-workers and classmates.

Left Out In America presents solid evidence that something's rotten in America. It stands as a disturbing example of what gets lost when we toss people onto the economic trash pile of this nation's warped family values. Pat's story will rattle the consciousness of our misguided and misrepresented government; it will rekindle compassion robust enough to overcome loathing for the fallen and forgotten; it will shine a light of courage in the quest to restore dignity and promise to her sisters and brothers of the streets. It's a campaign promise she's not forgotten, and Left Out is the rallying cry for those of us who believe in the promise of our pledge, "with liberty and justice for all."

Diane Nilan is the founder and president of HEAR US, Inc., a national organization dedicated to giving voice and visibility to homeless children and youth. Diane is a former homeless shelter director who sold her home and has been on the road since 2005 advocating for these children. Author and activist, Diane has also written a book on homelessness in the United States. Her book is called, *Crossing the Line: Taking Steps to End Homelessness*. More information is available at her website: www.hearus.us

PREFACE

I never intended to run for Vice President. Never.

Oh, sure, I toyed with the idea of becoming a Supreme Court Justice when I was about 10, but never, ever, did I consider VP. So you can imagine my surprise, when in 2004, I found myself traveling all across the United States of America trying to inspire and invigorate voters. If you are hurriedly checking the front of this book to see if I am John Edwards or Dick Cheney, let me save you some time.

Currently, I am the co-chair of the Green Party of the United States. But not that long ago I accompanied David Cobb as we ran for the highest offices in the land. 2004 was a crazy year. The country was as divided as the Red Sea, or mitochondria, depending on whether you hail from a red state or a blue state.

People who thought like me thought that the country needed a different president.

People who thought differently from me, thought that the Green Party was the reason that we didn't have one.

I was resolute that the Greens would not be the scapegoats again in 2004 and I worked diligently to that end. Ballot access laws in states all across the country require burgeoning parties to run candidates for president or else they must cease to exist. So when you are a small party, "you're damned if you do and damned if you don't."

Still, even though I knew we would lose party status all across the nation, I was advocating for no Presidential race.

I intended to remove the scapegoat from the discussion and expose the realities of the situation. I knew that as long as there was someone to blame, the real problems of the election of 2000 would never be corrected. And too many people in this world need the United States to have a fair and honest voting system.

I met with Ralph Nader the February afternoon before he announced that he would run for President in 2004. I asked him not to run. I agreed with him that 6 million Democrats voting for George Bush and corruption in Florida were the culprits, but I tried to impress upon him that the general public had a very different perception. I emphasized that political naiveté in the face of this pervasive sentiment might kill my party.

The following day he announced that he would run for President, but not as a Green.

Several weeks later I got a phone call from David Cobb. David, a Texas attorney recently transplanted to California, is a man that I greatly admire. The conversation went like this:

"Hey Pat, You know that I am running for nomination for the Green Party's presidential seat and I'd like you to consider being my running mate."

I replied, "David, I'm pretty public that I don't want to run anyone for President this year. I'm working diligently on this end to get the Party to stand aside. Please know that I'm honored and I think you are a great man and would be a fine standard-bearer for the party, but I think that this year we need to just sit this one out."

David respected this and asked if he might call again. I told him that it was always a pleasure to hear from him. And it was. And I did hear from him several more times as he worked to convince me to run. But when I finally did decide to run it wasn't what David Cobb said that persuaded me to toss my hat into the ring, but what all the others didn't say that made me do it.

By May, the major parties had settled upon their two candidates: The incumbent who had made the rich richer and devastated the assistance programs for the poor. He had marginalized the needs of women. He even stooped so low as to name a veterinarian as the national head of Women's Health!

And the challenger worked very diligently to sound just like him. I'm a journalist and a broadcaster by profession. So everyday I work reading the news. As winter turned to spring in 2004 I read little or nothing about the issues that mattered. Poverty, health care, families, the vanishing middle class, affordable housing – these issues were all overshadowed by name-calling and coward-baiting, by the war on terror and homeland security.

It had also become apparent that the Greens were definitely going to run a candidate. I was losing my battle to keep the Greens out of the national arena. My consolation prize was that I had the unique opportunity to shape the debate by becoming involved in the choice of the Presidential candidate: by becoming the Vice Presidential candidate.

As the country became more and more bitterly divided, it became horrifyingly clear that without our voices no one would speak to the grim realities that plagued the country.

Late May, I called David Cobb back.

"David, if I run will I be able to champion the causes I care about? Will I be able to stick up for families and kids and education and mommies and women's health and veterans and hunger and the elderly and illness and...."

David cut me off.

"Pat, that's why I want you to run."

Two months later, over the Fourth of July weekend, the campaign team met in Portland, Oregon, to strategize and plan the race. We identified local races around the country that we wanted to support. We identified key states where the presidential race was pretty much a done deal. We acknowledged our strengths and the issues we believed we could impact in the short time between Independence Day and voting day.

And we brainstormed ideas to highlight those things that mattered to us most.

At that meeting it was decided that I would live in 14 homeless shelters in 14 consecutive nights. We called it the "Left Out Tour" and this is its story.

INTRODUCTION

Living in homeless shelters sounds easy. After all, the homeless do it.

The stories in this book are their stories. You can decide if it's easy or not.

But as part of a Vice Presidential campaign, we had certain additional parameters to work into the experience. The committee for this part of the campaign set ground rules for the shelters we selected and for how we would execute this trip. The two weeks took more than two months to plan.

After we identified which states we wanted to include we had to make contact with supporters on the ground in each state.

I had volunteered at homeless shelters for years, and I was adamant that no homeless person should be displaced to accommodate my appearance.

We asked permission everywhere we went and didn't go where we weren't wanted.*

At one point during the 2004 campaign I was in Davenport, Iowa, at the same time that both Bush and Kerry were. They were both all over the local, national, and international news. The local newspaper covered my appearance.

Consequently, none of us believed that this tour would lead to some sort of media frenzy; but we also didn't want it to be exploitative for the sake of a political campaign. We needed to find a way to ensure that the local shelter benefited as much from our attendance as possible. If nothing else came of this attempt to highlight the existence of millions of homeless across the nation, we knew that we could at least fill the shelves of their pantries so that some positive impact would be felt.

So we collected necessities for each shelter that we attended. In Knoxville, Tennessee, it was bed sheets; in Chicago, Illinois, they needed toiletries. We attempted to discover the needs of the each shelter and use our local support to help fill those needs.

In the early part of the trip I managed to travel more as a homeless person than a national candidate. In fact one of my homeless companions hopped my train with me as I left New York and rode for a while before being discovered and ejected. As the distances became greater, we had to employ air travel rather than hitching a ride or hopping a bus. We had to obey a strict timetable. Each night I had another shelter to attend, generally by dark.

We adhered to every curfew and I did the chores required of shelter guests.

On a few occasions we had to abandon our first, second or even third choices for shelters in certain areas and the campaign staff would keep calling until they located one that would or could accept us. In most cases the shelters refused us because they were afraid that they would become politicized. Afraid that they would be punished for allowing a political candidate to come and stay. They feared losing their not-for-profit status or that powerful board members of different political background would become angry.

In several cases we changed our choice of shelter because the area shelters had waiting lines of dozens – in some cases, hundreds. In Boston, Massachusetts, we opted for sleeping in the street because there hadn't been an empty shelter bed for years.

In the case of the migrant farmers in Sonoma Valley, there had never been a shelter option. The workers just slept in the woods.

Only rarely was the media allowed in one of the shelters. Client privacy is guarded in these places and we took no pictures.

We stayed in public shelters and private shelters. We slept in churches and on sidewalks. We visited facilities that protected victims of domestic violence, or sheltered veterans or housed families with children. We also visited states where children are taken from parents who become homeless and others where moms and their babies slept in the same beds. I met hundreds of homeless babies, but never saw a shelter with a crib.

Possibly the most important thing to bear in mind while reading this book is that I am a journalist. And these are the stories as I witnessed them. I have never been homeless myself.

Even though as a kid we were poor and my family lived in a housing project in Providence, Rhode Island, I never felt at risk. If we had ever gotten close to homelessness, my mom never let it show.

I traveled with identification and a credit card for emergencies. I never feared producing my identification because my abuser would be able to find me. And when I lost my license in the very crowded Dulles International Airport just outside Washington, D.C., I had a staff of campaign workers to call and fix the problem.

I carried my belongings in a sack on my back, but I had carefully selected the items for this trip – it wasn't everything I owned. I had a cell phone and everyone from reporters to my children could make me feel part of a larger community with just a phone call.

There never came a day, or more importantly, a night that I couldn't walk away. Each moment, no matter how unbearable, I knew that I had a bed, a shower, a roof over my children's head and food in my cupboard. The clothes on my back got dirtier and dirtier, but I had a washer at home. Home. I had a home.

*The only shelter that we went to that didn't know we were coming was in New York City. The reasons for that deviance from protocol are explained in the chapters about New York.

AUGUSTA, MAINE

She drew my picture. When she was done, she took the crayon and scratched out the drawing of my face. I said, "Hey, what did you do that for? I drew a picture of you that was pretty." She stared at me like I made no sense. She actually seemed a little annoyed with my outburst. I picked up her pile of drawings to look at them; all of the faces were marked through. Cute little bodies, most with hands and feet, some complete with purses or shoes, but each and every drawing had the face of the person totally rubbed out with crayon.

"Who's that?" I asked, pointing to a tall drawing wearing a triangle skirt but no face.

"My mom," she smiled proudly.

"And this one, who is this one?"

"My baby." Of course, the baby's face was gone too.

Before I realized that her view of the world required her to remove all the faces, I had teased her about scratching my face off the page. When I did, she looked at me as if I had hurt her, offended her in some way. I tried to make amends. As we sat together at the table in the shelter, I tried to show her how I made my pictures. I showed her my drawings of her and her sister and that they had eyes and smiles. She only looked at me with the same puzzled expression. It appeared that she, at 4 years old, had long accepted the fact that there were folks who couldn't see faces the way that she did. Little Stephanie, the girl from the homeless shelter in Augusta, Maine, just knew that the faces of the people who dealt with her were dark and featureless. Her attitude was that she drew people as she saw them and she remained puzzled that others would be offended to have the reality of their non-existent features drawn for they themselves to see.

Stephanie was dirty. So was her baby sister. This was one of the few shelters I encountered where folks were not required to bathe.

I didn't know it at the time but this shelter, inside what used to be a single dwelling home in Maine's state capital, had very few rules compared with the other shelters in the country. Partly because of the shelter's policies and partly because of fewer state and local restrictions on shelters, the shelter's residents could make more personal choices.

Bathing, eating, and bedtimes were personal choices.

Families, for the most part had their own rooms and more privacy. And because this was a privately funded, very unique shelter in a rural state, without laws that took kids away from their homeless parents, kids were allowed to stay right in the same room with their parents.

Stephanie continued to color until her mom said she needed to go to bed. And except for her intense desire to color and the haunting nature of her pictures, Stephanie was easy-going and giggly. Her mom and I chatted as she drew pictures sitting between us. Her mom candidly related the circumstances that made her and her three kids leave home.

Dad was cruel and for safety sake, they needed to go.

This story repeated itself all across the country. Common also became the fact that all the kids weren't together in the same place. Stephanie had an older brother, not really grown up, just big enough to run away. Stephanie's mom hadn't seen her 10-year-old boy in almost a month. She thought he might have gone back to his dad. But because she was afraid of the man, she just couldn't know for sure.

This particular shelter was filled with moms and their children. It wasn't that way by design and it hadn't been that way all along.

It had started years earlier as an adult shelter. The mostly male population had, over the past five years or so, given way almost entirely to families. On this particular night there weren't any men at all.

There was a pregnant girl, about 23, whose boyfriend had tried to get her to terminate the pregnancy. She ran away from him so that she could have the baby.

There were several working moms. As the night wore on, they trickled in from their jobs, with their kids. There is no daycare at the shelter, so working homeless moms need to find a place for their kids to go. Some went to friends' houses. Others didn't go anywhere special. Some even waited outside the buildings where their parents worked. For safety's sake and because of the unknown nature of the residents' background and character, it's against shelter policy for the guests to baby-sit for each other. So the kids can't go home, eat, or start their homework, until their folks get out of work.

The resident moms made an exception that night I was there, and the attendant looked the other way. There was a mom who had gone to party. The shelter didn't allow anyone who had been using alcohol or drugs to stay there. When the folks are intoxicated they have to find alternative lodging, consequently so do their children.

This one particular woman had a couple of toddlers. They sat in the back of the cab with her when she arrived back at the house. The attendant couldn't let her in; she staggered and swayed.

The women standing there when the partying mom arrived helped the kids out of the cab and circled the kids like a protective pack. They sent the mom away and kept the kids there with them. They struggled to divert the attention of the shelter attendant finally having to invent an explanation of why they had kept the kids and broken the rules.

The concern that kids are easy prey in the company of strangers lies at the root of the policy that kids can't stay without their folks. The women, the shelter staff, every person there acknowledged the liability of kids staying without their mom, but on this particular night, they more keenly identified the danger of letting them go with her.

The shelter attendant likely knew that they were lying. And while they knew the truth, no one spoke it. For safety's sake, the toddlers slept soundly on the couch that night, where everyone could see them and where everyone could watch everyone else.

The transient nature of living in a shelter evaporated for a few moments. It felt so much like a family protecting its own, but if I had gone back a week later, most of these people would be gone. These women who had never seen each other a month earlier would never see each other again one month later.

Stephanie, her baby sister and her mom went to bed. By then, a whole new crop of kids and parents had filled the kitchen. I helped several of the older kids with their homework. Two middle-school-aged boys had never lived in a shelter until that month. You could tell the boys liked each other. They stood as bookends ready to guard from either side. They clearly liked their mom too, and they accepted their situation with good humor while their mom worked to sort out their lives.

She had served in the Air Force and later became a Reservist. When she got called up to go to Iraq, she obediently left her job and reported for duty. If her family wanted to stay with her until she left, they had to relocate to the area of her pre-deployment duty. Her husband was angry; he didn't want to follow her through the motions of becoming an activated member of the Air Force once again, and refused to go. When she agreed that she should go alone, he refused to have sole responsibility for the children and packed his things and left.

While she and the boys struggled to accept all these changes; she brought the kids with her and reported for active duty. Maybe dad would miss them, maybe he would reconsider, maybe he would see that the kids needed him when she went overseas, or maybe the Air Force would consider keeping her stateside because she was the only family her boys had.

A 35-year-old smoker and a former pencil pusher in the service who had limited physical prowess, she blew out her knee her sixth week into the re-training program. The military discharged her. When she called her husband to tell him, he didn't want her back.

When I met them, she and the boys had been at the shelter for almost a month; nigh on a record for longevity in Augusta. The shelter has a months-long waiting list and the staff tries to get folks going a lot quicker than that. But this particular resident was gainfully employed with a plan for getting her feet back under her. While this mom worked and saved enough money to get a first and last month's rent, the shelter accommodated them and let them stay.

With the military's discharge her military pay had been severed. They weren't getting any voluntary help from the father. There was no child support order; there hadn't even been a divorce yet. As for the government stepping in, when motivating no longer financially supportive parents to pay for their kids, the courts require considerably longer than a few weeks.

In the Air Force, our G I Jane had done clerical work. Similar work does not pay well in Maine. Add to that her transient status, and you don't have a recipe for a high-paying job, or a quick trip out of the shelter. Telemarketing had recently become the fastest-growing industry in Maine. Still at $8 or even $10 an hour saving $1,000 would take a while.

Undaunted and needing bigger paychecks, this Jane found much more lucrative work: The highest paid form of telemarketing. She was bright, articulate, well spoken and had a great laugh. She got a job selling sex.

Porn magazine subscriptions, marital aids, sex toys, videos, you name it. The more she upsold, the higher her pay. She knew that in about two more weeks she would have the money for a place of her own. And she was extra lucky. She was only recently down and out, so she still had her car. Without the car, she never would've gotten back and forth to work.

Jane's boys both had coughs. The one consistent reality of each and every shelter I stayed in was the raspy wet cough that echoed through the night.

The kitchen of the shelter had a long table, about eight chairs, and at the far end a couple of couches and a television set. These were the couches upon which the drunken woman's children would sleep, where the middle school boys did their homework, and above which the signs cautioning about tuberculosis were hung.

"Consumption" it had been called at the turn of the 20th century. It had been proclaimed that this "wasting disease" had been eradicated in the United States in our lifetimes. But now tuberculosis is back all across the country. In prisons, shelters, on the street, either the disease itself or the fear of it hangs with every gravelly soggy cough you hear.

As they struggled to control their coughing, I worried about the boys; I worried about the other kids. You could see it in the eyes of the other moms too. We all worried.

Earlier that day we had held a press conference to announce the beginning of the Left Out Tour, the name for my trip around the country living with the homeless. The governor and members of the Maine State Housing Authority had convened a meeting inside the Augusta Civic Center to discuss homelessness. So we had our press conference outside.

The folks inside the civic center who worked to deal with the issues of poverty, a lack of affordable housing, and the corresponding homelessness didn't come to our conference, but the homeless did. A mom and her high-school-aged son held signs saying, "homelessness sucks" and they meant it. The son really meant it.

It was early afternoon when most high-school-aged boys are in high school. Craig, a freshman, had dropped out a few weeks earlier. For the time being at least, he had his mom's blessing. They were both tired of him being beaten up.

Craig had never been the most popular kid in school. For the most part, however, he managed to stay under the radar.

When he and his mom lost their housing and moved into the shelter, Craig had walked the two or so miles to his old school bus stop so that the other kids wouldn't know. It was a nuisance – but, he thought, a worthwhile one.

One day he had to leave early. The shelter has an unmarked van solely for the purpose of disguising the reality of the young people's living conditions. Still, the shelter staff has to provide proof of permission to collect kids at the schools, and as a result the school staff learns where the kids are going.

Stupidity, naiveté, casual disregard, or meanness: something motivated the office staff to page Craig and say that the home-less shelter bus was waiting for him.

Fresh meat for the bullies: let the beatings begin.

So Craig was at the press conference, with his mom, holding his sign, meaning every word of it.

It was a pretty autumn day. Stephanie's mom had brought her and her baby sister to the event as well. Craig watched over them and played with them. He kept them entertained for hours while everyone waited for the important people, the powerful people inside the civic center to come out to acknowledge them, or to stay inside and fix the problem.

They are still waiting.

In the year 2004, the Bread of Life Ministries in Augusta had already helped more than 400 people by the time they housed me. Tragically, they had sent more than 700 away.

Most of the folks who had stayed there in those first nine months had been families. A few singles; but no single teens. Single teens are too vulnerable; they come with such an assort-ment of problems and needs that there is no shelter for them in Augusta at all.

When homeless teens present themselves in the area, they are sent away. Teens go to other cities in other places. They go to more urban places. They give up their friends, their familiar sur-roundings, their teachers, their neighbors and what little support network they may have in place to go to a group home, or to live on the street, and share the company of other unpredictable teens.

Coincidentally, the keynote speaker at the conference outside of which our press conference was held, was a young woman who herself had been made homeless when her parents died
in a car accident. She, as a homeless teen, had prevailed. Ironically, she told the tales of her successes in a town that sends its
homeless teens away.

HARRIET TUBMAN

I slept that night on the bottom bunk in the single women's room on the first floor. The beds were made of rough-hewn 2x6s and had twin mattresses. There were three of us in a room that held four. The final bunk was the only empty bed in the house. Except, of course, for the ones that should have held the partying momma and her children.

The shelter provided bedding that I could have used but I brought my own sleeping bag and a pillow. I didn't want to dirty their sheets.

When I left home for this trip, I packed one small bag of clothes and I had a sack with my sleeping bag and pillow in it. Needing to travel light, I didn't bring any clothing that I would have been upset to lose.

In my pocket I had one credit card for emergencies and my driver's license so that I could travel. Since Sept. 11, 2001, it has become virtually impossible to travel without identification. Travelers have to show their ID to board a bus or a train. This poses an increased liability to many people who wind up homeless; especially, those fleeing from abusive relationships.

People flow into the information stream with great ease. Once in the databases of the various transportation systems, someone's location becomes easy to track. A person with a modicum of computer savvy can track down just about anyone.

Because I didn't mind carrying my ID and credit card I used the trains and planes available to move between locations. But if I had wanted to hide for any reason, I would have had to stick to far less safe methods of transport, like hitchhiking or stowing away.

When we got up the following morning, the residents asked me to stay. Although we had been up most of the night talking, they had more to say.

I couldn't stay; I had to get to my next shelter. And they had to get to work. And their kids had to get to school. Donated food lined the kitchen walls. The kids had cereal and milk and collected their things for the bus. G.I. Jane offered me a ride. She was driving her kids to the school bus stop. If they stuck with their familiar bus stop, maybe none of the other kids would catch on that they didn't live in their old apartment anymore.

The boys probably could have walked to the bus stop, but frost had gathered on the windows and the boys had those nasty coughs. She offered to take me where I needed to go, but I didn't want her wasting a drop of gasoline taking me out of her way, so I just hopped out at the bus stop too.

A group of other kids had already gathered at the stop, and they yelled comments and greetings to the boys. You could really see how much Jane loved her sons and I admired her desire to keep their lives as normal as possible. Luckily for Jane, she was a fighter, in a situation where she still had some tools with which to fight. I wanted to go to a phone, call her husband, ask him why he couldn't be more of a dad. I doubted that I would've gotten much of an answer. And I didn't know his name. And anyway, I had to start walking. I had to get to Boston.

I left my car at the civic center where we had held the press conference. I walked about a mile and a half to get to it. Along the way a Portland, Maine, talk radio station interviewed me via the phone. I stood on the side of a very busy commuter road – trucks whizzing by, kicking road grit up at me, with everything

I had to live for the next two weeks slung onto my back – and I tried explain why what I was doing mattered.

The Associated Press had just released the statistics that 800,000 more kids lived in poverty in 2004 than in 2003, and that 1.2 million more folks in the United States had no health insurance. The total number of those without health insurance now topped 45 million. Our country's great divide between the haves and the have nots had grown enormously and that trend showed no signs of slowing, let alone reversing.

I told the radio host that it was no wonder the shelter was full. People in our country languish in poverty. They struggle and by the millions they lose the struggle.

I explained that I had just spent the night with dozens of homeless folks and not one of them appeared to use drugs or showed any signs of mental illness. All but one of the adults had a job. And anecdotally speaking, in little old Augusta, Maine, for every one person I spent the night with, there were one and a half more turned away from shelter.

Then one of the radio talk show hosts, with a rather sardonic tone asked, "What do you think we can do about it? What do you expect your two weeks of living with these people to do."

I responded, "Maybe we could just look at it. Maybe we could just start there. Stare at the problem instead of looking away. Look at the minimum-wage jobs that contribute to the problem, look at the lack of health care, look at the lack of affordable housing. Look in the mirror and calculate how much time anyone of us could live without one of these things before we realize that 'they' could be 'us.'"

The radio host sounded mildly amused by the notion of recognizing the problems of homelessness, but seemed to feel that the issues were basically the problems of the homeless' own making.

I'd only lived in one shelter; I hadn't amassed enough experience to adequately explain what I had begun to feel. Soon enough I would learn to articulate the scourge homelessness is to all of society, to explain that it is the threat of losing our homes and cars and families that keeps us working for sub-standard wages, living in the only industrialized nation without health care for all its citizens; keeps us living too close to the edge. Fear of being the next inhabitants in the world of soup kitchens and charity clothing oppresses and controls us all.

I hadn't witnessed enough reality to see that even if we never become homeless ourselves, the price to society as a whole remains enormous. I felt it inside, but I could not yet articulate it. It had only been one night, in a rural and peaceful shelter, where tuberculosis, while frightening, remained the only villain in the dark. I had 13 nights to go. I would learn more.

I finished the interview, I continued to walk up the hill toward my car, and I thought of the great heroine, Harriet Tubman. Harriet Tubman ran the Underground Railroad prior to the United States Civil War. She shuttled blacks out of the South to safety in the North. Ms. Tubman once said, "If I could have convinced more slaves that they were slaves, I would have freed thousands more." I'd wished she had done the interview.

CAMBRIDGE, MASSACHUSETTS

I went to college in Boston – well, Chestnut Hill actually. The front of the BC brochure said, "Boston College, not in Boston, not a college."

What a great city: Boston. Trolley lines to take you anywhere you could possibly want to go. Fenway Park, Fanueil Hall, Old Ironsides, churches, art galleries, plays, restaurants, diversity. Boston just has everything.

My freshman year at BC the tuition was $3,000; the trolley was 25 cents. Today the trolley is a buck, BC's tuition $32,000. This disproportionate increase isn't due to inflation; it's a result of investment... well, lack of investment, really. Federal contribution to higher education has been cut by 80 percent since 1980.

In 1978, the U.S. government invested in people. Our leaders, our doctors, our lawyers, many, if not most, had been educated by the G.I. Bill, a government program to educate the folks who fought in World War II and in Korea. The G.I. Bill turned out to be the best investment ever made by the U.S. federal government. The educated vets paid far more back in taxes on their increased earnings than they ever could have paid working as uneducated labor. But by the 1980s the lessons of the G.I. Bill became legends. And government funding for education all but vanished.

We used to take the trolley to Cambridge back in my days at BC. We would get cool posters at the Harvard Coop, parade around dropping half sentences when stuffy looking people walked by, like, "Did you hear from Uncle Teddy. Is he still picking us up on his way from Hyannis?" And we'd laugh like crazy when the stuffy folks turned their heads to see who said those things. We might as well have been saying, "In 25 years when I am running for Vice President, I think I'll come sleep in these streets and see what I can learn from the folks who live the American Nightmare. In fact, I'll be one of 10 million homeless people on the streets of the United States on that particular night." Oh, what am I thinking: We would never have said that. Say what you want about Uncle Teddy, we thought then that he and the voters would never let things get that bad.

It was really easy to get to Harvard Square from BC: Green Line to the Red Line and the Red Line right smack dab to the center of Cambridge. Up from the underground to a place I now know is called "the pit." It's a lot like a comic book character: By day, a simple Red Line station; by night, a homeless hangout. My night in Boston, we went there on purpose. First, the allure of witnessing something that seems so alien, the homeless social scene; and second, it was the night that the free clinic van saw sick transients.

Right there, not five football fields from the statue of John Harvard, a half a walk away from swank little eateries and my old haunt, the Harvard Coop, the van waited. It looked like a cross between an infirmary and an ice cream truck, the brightly colored drawings of smiling kids and rocket cones mysteriously missing from the sides of the van. And once it drove into place, folks from nowhere appeared at its window.

Emaciated, filthy, sore-covered, pleading individuals whose appearances made me gasp approached for help. Some of them amazingly managed to stand and wait. They looked so frail. And in spite of the fact that they didn't seem strong enough to hold themselves up, the clientele waited and did so, politely.

Inside the health-care van the lights were so bright that the silhouettes of the sick folks stood dark in the night against the brightly lit folks inside who tried to help them. One woman –

she couldn't have weighed more than a hundred pounds and she must have been nearly 6 feet tall – carried this raggedy bag with what appeared to be clothes and personal items in it. She was given some medicine; she put it in her bag. She was told to stay warm. A reporter for the Boston Metro came up to talk to me. When I turned back, she was gone.

I had stepped into the circle of life. Living on the street makes you sick. Being sick makes you live on the street.

ROSIE'S PLACE

Earlier in the day, I had been at an outreach center for homeless teens called Youth on Fire. I met with counselors and advocates who themselves hadn't yet turned 25 and they worked with these teens to help them, to try and get them jobs or homes, and to give them advice. Unfortunately, the statistics they gave me showed that these kids came for help way too late.

A handsome African-American man in his early 20s sat with a fruit bowl of condoms on the side of his desk and explained to me that 30 percent of Boston's 14-to-24-years-old kids are HIV-positive. I thought these statistics are way too high. But even if he only meant homeless teens, the numbers are horrific.

Staggering, I asked how it could be. He explained that drugs, the sex trade, loneliness, the plagues of the young, gave way to the plague of the century.

Another care worker and teen advocate explained that when kids live on the street they have very little with which to barter. Their bodies become their only commodity.

Youth on Fire supplied computers for the kids to get on the Internet or write resumes. The table in the middle of the room had snacks for them to eat. The fairly large room gave shelter during the day, but was off limits at night. At the far end sat the counselors working diligently to help any kid they could. On certain days the kids could get to see a nurse there as well. But when darkness fell they all had to get out and look for a place to stay.

Outside the day shelter, there were some young people waiting. Most of these kids had homes, some had been homeless, a couple of Harvard students who had dedicated much of their free time to working with poverty, hunger, and healthcare issues sat and waited as well. One young woman had a tape recorder. She was a communications student and had a radio show on the local community station. She interviewed me about running for Vice President while I asked her questions about the homeless situation in the area.

When some of the local Green Party members showed up for our, 'leave the situation better than we found it' part of the day, we took off for Rosie's Place. Our community service in Boston brought us to the first-ever soup kitchen in the United States designed exclusively for women.

Gil, our contact through the Greens, had made our arrangements. He went to the man that we needed to see, who put us to work. The guy who seemed to be running the place was a giant burly African-American man, probably about 40 years old with a kind smile. He nodded his greeting to us and then gave us aprons and put us to work. First, we had to wash and dry our hands and put on rubber gloves.

One of the young women from the grass outside of Youth on Fire, a tiny little pretty girl with black dreadlocks and a tight tank-top put on her apron and her rubber gloves. She looked a lot like a delicate Bob Marley preparing to ladle soup.

The food looked and smelled great. A half a dozen or so other volunteers worked on the meal already. Folks chopped fresh vegetables for salad or sauce. About 12 people worked on the meal. The big guy handed us ladles and a pot containing about 5 gallons of chicken noodle soup. Everything was freshly made. No canned food. We barely got settled when the women started to arrive.

At first it was a trickle, then they began to pour into the dining hall. So many that after a while I became too busy to watch the line grow. I was busy ladling as Marley doled out crackers.

Some women asked for no broth, some extra broth, some extra crackers, some no crackers: all very polite. Some women asked for more than one bowl. We didn't ask why and I was too busy to look up or care why – we just gave it to them.

I started thinking that maybe some women would get only soup while others would get the sauce dish being prepared behind my back and the soup eaters feared that they would be too hungry with just one bowl of soup, but they had to chose one or the other, and having chosen soup, they wanted to have enough.

I was wrong.

The soup vanished in a half hour or so. Marley and I went out into the large L-shaped dining room to collect dirty plates and cups so that they could be washed for reuse during the next part of the meal. As we walked out among the women, I learned why so many had asked for an extra bowl. Sure, some of the women had gotten soup for the elderly women around them, but I had misunderstood the term "women's shelter." I had assumed it had been designed for only women. But there I stood in a dining room that was teaming with children. Of course! A shelter for women would be full of children.

Little homeless kids played and talked and ate in the company of their homeless moms. One whole section of the 200-plus-person dining room had child-height tables and chairs. One wall, lined with bookcases stood filled with children's books. Before they return to the streets, a nice little story could be read to the kids, or by the kids, who had accompanied their moms for a hot meal.

The sight of all those kids stunned me. I asked one of the volunteers why there weren't any boys over the age of 10 or so. "Oh, they aren't allowed to come in here. Boys that old aren't allowed in here at all. Sometimes you'll see them wait outside for their moms to bring them something. But mostly they have to go to the men's shelters. They aren't allowed." My heart sank. How chilling: a 12-year-old boy in a shelter for men.

A flamboyantly dressed and colorful lady came bounding up to me and another volunteer, Crystal. Crystal had spent many years living on the streets in New Hampshire, Massachusetts and New York; she had volunteered to help me get acquainted on the streets of Boston and Cambridge. As Crystal and I cleared the tables, this highly animated woman bounded over to us and hugged Crystal tightly. They had been homeless together for many months. They had shared the same streets and alleys trying to find a place to sleep.

Crystal and her friend avoided the shelters. Crystal simply hated the shelters. For her friend, it wasn't about preference; it was about survival.

As the two spoke I started to notice the darkness of the woman's skin around her lips and cheeks and chin. Crystal's friend had a strong Hispanic accent and had come to this part of the country several years back seeking work and acceptance. Although small in stature, her hands and arms had large bones and appeared strong.

When they finished speaking, Crystals friend walked away, so happy to have had a few minutes to catch up with her old friend. After she walked away I asked if my suppositions were correct. "Yes," confirmed Crystal, "she's a transvestite. She doesn't technically belong here but she'll get pounded senseless in the men's shelters. None of the women mind. The women's shelters and soup kitchens are really the only places safe for gay men and transgender folks. She's safe here."

In Boston the term "woman" doesn't just mean "woman." It means "child," it means "vulnerable man," it means "accepting of others." Consequently, sadly, dangerously, "pubescent boy" means "man."

I stood there, trying to get my mind around the idea that the little kids and old ladies had to go back outside to sleep after dinner, that three out of four of the young women I looked at had HIV, and that I stood surrounded by those most easily preyed upon in our society. And I wondered how I had known so little about them all just an hour earlier. As I absentmindedly wandered through the dining room, clearing the dishes from the tables, I became lost in my own thoughts.

That's when the lady whose bowl of soup I had taken away, thinking she had finished with it, yelled at me and brought me back to earth. I jumped.

Seems they have a system, one that no one had explained to me. If you need to get up and chase your kid around the dining hall or get a drink of milk, or run to the bathroom, you make this little tent out of the napkin and put it on your plate. That way the well-meaning folks who volunteer don't take your food away. No one told me, I took her soup, and there was no more left with which I could replace it.

Thankfully, there was another dish to serve. I just hoped that the woman liked spaghetti.

We started serving the pasta, the male volunteers had taken over doing the dishes, and I began to wonder how I was gonna make it through 12 more days.

After we fed the people from the street, we stood at the counter from which they had been served and ate as well. It was possibly the most solemn meal of my life. No one spoke, no one smiled. The lack of mirth seemed odd, after all we were doing good things, but the grim reality that we lived only in that moment and had no effect on the future hung between us as we ate. Our guests would leave the warm, well-lit, yummy-smelling kitchen to return to the bleak world that had sent them there in the first place.

And not one of us could do anything about it.

A woman from the back office asked Crystal and me to help her sort donated toiletries. We sat in a small back room with boxes and boxes of hotel soaps and shampoos and samples of make up sorting them into categories. All the nail files, all the razors, even those little plastic two-bladed razors had to be thrown away. We couldn't give them anything that they could use to hurt themselves.

Later in the trip as I boarded planes to travel across the country I would remember that the same items were removed from our carry-on bags. Affluent or poor, somewhere along the way, we'd stopped trusting that people would not hurt each other or themselves.

As we sorted through the items a woman worked on a computer behind us. We learned that she actually worked at Rosie's Place. She explained that all the others working in the kitchen had volunteered from a local church. The 22nd of each month had long been the night that this particular group spent feeding the guests at Rosie's place. This volunteer team brought in all the food with them. They cooked everything from scratch. They had never been reimbursed. And every night of the month a different group did the same.

As we left, I went to use the restroom. Back to the real world.

The kitchen and dining area had been a respite from the true homeless existence.

Once down the hallway I returned to surroundings that would grow more familiar with each day that I spent living with the homeless. The homeless world is filled with disease, filth and anger.

Someone had been horribly ill in the restroom.

The women fought over who should clean the mess. They fought over who had made the mess. No one wanted to clean a mess that wasn't their's. One by one the women walked away and just left the nastiness, the filth where they had found it.

I started sensing a theme. If you walk away from something nasty, it ceases to exist.

In less than 48 hours, my homeless life was becoming a metaphor for the world that contained, created and consequently sustained it. I thought about how easy it is to ignore the scourge of poverty and disease.

Then I caught my first homeless condition. I got mad.

LOTTERY

Have you ever played the lottery? I have, but only a handful of times. I played those huge jackpot big money drawing games. Who knows? I might have become a millionaire a time or two, except that I've never held onto the ticket long enough to see if I actually won. The outcome of the lottery just never seemed that important.

In Boston, being homeless can be a full-time job. And it's mostly because of the lottery.

After we left Rosie's Place we traveled up by the Fleet Center. I hadn't been there since the big sporting arena had been the Boston Garden. And now some other bank has bought the name from Fleet, but the night we were there, it was still called the Fleet center. Now that names of public place get sold for advertising, I find it harder to remember the names.

Crystal had set up a tour of one of the larger shelters for us. It hung in the shadow of the highway just before it descended and disappeared below the surface of the city, as part of Boston's "Big Dig" underground road system. The shelter was quite large. They had a women's building and a men's building.

We toured the women's facility. The men's side didn't allow us past the front lobby. Crystal had done her prep work and they knew we were coming, but between the time we got there and when we were going to look around, one of the men getting frisked on his way in produced a length of pipe and a fist fight had begun. They asked us to leave so that we wouldn't get hurt.

This particular facility had metal detectors and they searched everyone. One of the attendants told us that they collected weapons every night. He couldn't remember a night without at least one confiscation.

The atmosphere around the corner at the women's facility lacked all that explicit violent tone. The women, like the men, had just begun to file into the building. No metal detector on this side and no frisking: just a desk at which guests stopped and produced their lottery number and their identification. No hiding allowed at this particular shelter.

Every morning the shelter gave out numbers for that evening. If a person hoped to sleep there on a given night, that person had to arrive earlier the same day and pick up a lottery ticket. The line formed hours before the numbers were distributed and it consumed a major part of the day to ensure that an individual would get shelter that night. Residence there on a prior night did not ensure that there would be a place to stay the following night.

In the evening, those with the lottery numbers re-formed a line again. Many people with numbers too high to actually get into the shelter would show up anyway, hoping that someone with a lower number didn't make it back that night. The shelter attendant who gave us our tour said that she didn't know how anyone could have a job and still have time to qualify for a place to sleep. Crystal told me that they don't. It's one or the other.

I filed into the building with the "lottery winners" and went through the same paces that the guests undergo. The building, large and brightly painted, had furnishings on the first floor similar to a college dorm lobby; with a touch of bus depot security measures thrown in to assure that no one walked off with a table or chair. High in the corners of the lobby hung a couple of television screens. Women sat watching television while others came and went through a secure door in the back to the smoking area. No second-hand smoke in the shelters in Boston – tuberculosis maybe, but no smoke.

Upstairs, the women were given bedding. The rooms were like those of the "Madeline" books, with the girl's dormitory of long slender beds, one after the other, lining the walls. After dropping the bedding on the cot of their choice, the women were given small amounts of soap and shampoo and they showered. Many of the shelters across the country have this rule, mandatory showers to stay in their facility.

I turned from the line where the women with naked shoulders, freshly washed and wrapped in towels, waited to use the sinks to brush their teeth and I saw an elderly woman struggling to put the sheets on her bed. Instinctively I went over to help her make the bed. Unbeknownst to me, Crystal took off after me to stop me, but not in time.

I stooped and asked this tiny frail-looking woman, her skin as white and transparent as her hair, if I could help her. She lunged at me.

"Don't touch my bed!"

I leapt back. She glared, her teeth bared and her face contorted with anger.

Stunned into wide-eyed staring I just stood there, unmoving, amazed by the fury and the vicious way that she had spat the words at me. Crystal had made it to my side by then and took my arm. The old woman turned her angry face to Crystal and said, "Get her away from me. You, too, get away from me."

TUXEDO

He sang as he approached us. His beautiful baritone voice made us all turn around and look. Light on his feet, dressed in a black tuxedo with white shirt and tie, sporting a lapel almost bent over with the weight of a large sprig of white flowers, an elderly black man came upon us, having what seemed to be the most delightful night of his life.

Upon closer inspection (we inspected him, he seemed not to notice us) we could better see the details of his attire. Filth covered the man, from the top of his dark gray hair to the tips of his battered black sneakers. The flowers he sported from his jacket were plastic and his tie and collar were badly frayed. If desperation had a dress code, here stood the trendsetter himself.

The moment possessed a magical quality. A sublime fanciful nature surrounded the scene as the fellow cruised by us, singing with an orchestra we couldn't hear, completely impervious to our existence.

Then suddenly, like a lightning bolt striking the brick square where we sat, two cruel and violent young men sprang at the gentleman, nearly knocking him to the ground. The night was so dark and the man had so completely captivated our attention that these hoodlums virtually materialized out of sheer nothingness.

They brutishly assaulted the man. Insulting him, shoving him, taunting him: pulling at his clothes and knocking him around.

Four or five of the local homeless young people had joined us again that evening. We had planned to find a piece of ground to sleep on, as the shelters in the area had reached their capacity. We had returned to the Pit, where we gathered earlier in the day to watch the health-care wagon treat transients. The Pit each night served as a rendezvous point for homeless teens that wanted to meet. Once the streets got deserted we had planned to go find a safe place to stay.

The Red Line subway station, chameleon of Harvard Square, had changed yet again. The Pit had transformed earlier from subway stop to homeless hangout, then to health clinic, and in that moment it had turned into boxing ring. More than a boxing ring, it was an arena for predatory violence, where modern-day gladiators lashed out at the vulnerable old man.

Once I processed that these big young bullies had plans to more than humiliate this old man, once the two or three young homeless youths sitting next to me realized that I would back them up if they defended the old man, we rose to our feet.

All at once the scene escalated and grew frenzied. Before we could make it across the pit to where the old man cried, yelled and threw punches in his own defense, two more great big men jumped into the fray. They had sticks drawn and they yelled fiercely and we all froze again in shock, right where we stood.

To the average passerby, Harvard Square appears adequately lit. Traffic lights and streetlights illuminate the area and it doesn't seem dark or remote. But something about the intensity of the circumstances made it seem that everything but where this violent scene unfolded hung in the darkness and became invisible.

That's why none of us, not me and my homeless companions, not the dapper old dodger, not the bullies, not anybody, saw the police when they pulled their cruiser onto the square.

The big men with the big voices and the big sticks were Cambridge's finest: and not a moment too soon.

One of the officers had a voice that shattered all the other sounds. The cries of the old man, the taunts of the young men, every sound ceased at the moment that he boomed his commands to the brutes.

"Take your hands off him. Who the fuck do you think you are? You think you can fuck with him like that? Well, you can't fuck with anybody like that." He grabbed the larger of the young men and threw him across the square. The bully jogged to get his legs to catch up with the speed that the policeman had given to his upper body. The bully ran head first toward a telephone pole. He brought his arms out in front of him, just in time, grabbing the pole with his hands and steadying himself there.

The other policeman grabbed hold of the smaller bully and twisted his arm behind his back. We continued closing the distance between the old man and ourselves. His clothes had been pulled out of shape. He was hunched over and swearing and sputtering. As he stooped, he struggled to tuck his shirt back into his pants and square his now misshapen collar. He saw the police pushing the hoodlums up against the bulletin boards that stood in the square. The old man looked at them and yelled at them. He just kept yelling at the kids, yelling at the cops, yelling at them all.

As we approached to help him, he turned to us struggling with his composure and told us to stay away, to leave him alone. We obeyed. He smoothed his clothes some more and walked off in the direction that he had originally been heading. Mirth gone, magical moment gone, he walked away stripped of his fanciful nature. Nothing left but the reality that his tuxedo and his flowers and his singing had only briefly taken away.

every sound ceased at the moment that he barked his commands to the brutes.

"Take your hands off him. Who the fuck do you think you
are? You think you can fuck with him like that? Well, you can't
fuck with anybody like that." He grabbed the larger of the young
men and threw him across the square. The bully jogged to get his
legs to catch up with the speed that the policeman had given to
his upper body. The bully ran first head first toward a telephone pole.
He brought his arms out in front of him, just in time, grabbing
the pole with his hands and steadying himself there.

The other policeman grabbed hold of the smaller bully and
twisted his arm behind his back. We continued closing the distance between the old man and ourselves. His clothes had been
pulled out of shape. He was hunched over and swearing and
sputtering. As he stooped, he struggled to tuck his shirt back
into his pants and square his now-misshapen collar. He saw the
police pushing the hoodlums up against the bulletin boards that
stood in the square. The old man looked at them and yelled at
them. He just kept yelling at the kids, yelling at the cops, yelling
at them all.

As we approached to help him, he turned to us, shrugging
with his composure and told us to stay away, to leave him alone.
We obeyed. He smoothed his clothes some more and walked off
in the direction that he had originally been heading. With gone,
magical moment gone, he walked away stripped of his fanciful
nature. Nothing left but the reality that his tuxedo and his flowers and his singing had only briefly taken away.

LADY VICE PRESIDENT

"The cops let 'em go. They let 'em go. How da ya like that? If that had a been me, they'da arrested me. They didn't arrest those white kids."

Ron, one of our companions for the evening wasn't really complaining about what happened. His sentences were more declarative than plaintive. Ron, 30 years old with a Denzel Washington kind of handsome looks, had lived on the streets of Boston as a young man. Now he worked with the area youths a couple of nights a week and he tried to help them make different choices.

When Ron heard that a Vice Presidential candidate wanted to sleep with the homeless youths of Boston, he showed up out of sheer disbelief. When I moved to go and help the old man, he had been right beside me. Later, he told me that he got up with me to stop me.

"Those punks woulda beat on you just like the old man. They wouldn't a cared."

It all worked out OK, the police had arrived, they saved the old man, but then they let the bullies go.

We started wandering the deserted streets. Crystal took me to a Staples office supply store where the manager had a reputation for being nice to the local kids and didn't mind if we used the bathroom. I brushed my teeth. I'd only been gone two days and these basic routines had already begun to feel out of place.

After we left the bathroom, Crystal took me to part of the store with vibrating chairs. The cushions had a back rubbing devise. As the machine hummed and rubbed my torso and legs, I felt more tired than I ever had in my life. But not the more tired than I was going to feel over the next 12 days.

After our little respite we returned to the street and walked back to the group. The late September evening had turned cold and we needed to find a place to stay. Other folks looking for accommodations had already taken all the good spots. According to Crystal the little entryways to storefronts make great sleeping areas in the cold because they block the wind and the close quarters keep your body heat from escaping too quickly.

We turned onto the campus of Harvard. Harvard College: the nation's oldest institution of higher learning. Harvard College, where President George W. Bush, got his MBA.

We wandered through the campus courtyards and alleyways. We peered into the empty lobbies at empty couches in heated foyers. One of the teens yelled that he had found the perfect spot.

Nestled in the elbow of a building, where the outer wall turned a corner, was a patch of loose soil. Crystal agreed: a perfect location. Turns out that soft earth makes a much better mattress than concrete.

It occurred to me that I had the only sleeping bag. I opened it and laid it out on the ground. I apologized that it wouldn't keep anyone warm but it might keep us dry. Ron said, "Haven't you ever heard of a 'homeless blanket'? Nobody gets to be shy when it's cold."

He lay down next to me and put his arms around me and said, "Come on everybody, let's keep her warm." Then the other kids all came and lay down with us. We all hung onto each other. They all took turns telling what their lives had been like. Why they ended up on the street. Who they knew that got off the street or who died there. Some spoke of things at home that were unspeakable. Every one of them had a memory that would have been better forgotten.

A policeman came by about 1 a.m. He told us that he didn't mind us being there as long as we didn't "bust anything up" or make too much noise. Then he told us, "Good night."

About 3 a.m. a private security guard came by and started screaming at us. He stood up on the courtyard 50 or so feet from the elbow of the building against which we settled.

Huddled together we had fallen asleep and now this man's screams had frightened us awake. The man sounded unstable. He screamed obscenities at us and told us we had to leave. I don't know why I felt the way I did, but I lay there convinced that he would pull his gun and shoot us. The tone of his voice made the air turn bitter cold, despite the homeless blanket.

Frenetic, exasperated, he ran off down the street and called the cops.

When the policeman arrived it was the same one who had told us that we could stay. He said, "You gotta get outta here now. You can't stay. I know I told you you could, but now you can't. I got this security guard here breakin' my balls and he wants you out, so now you gotta get out. I'm sorry kids, but you gotta go."

Crystal stood up and tried to discuss it with him. Maybe because he had been so nice to us, she thought she could explain our reason for being there and he would understand.

Crystal shouted back to him, "See this lady. She's running for Vice President. She's here because she's trying to learn what it's like to be left out in America. She's running for Vice President. She's going all over the country doing this. She's Pat..."

Crystal's voice trailed off as we tried to stop her from going on with the story. Crystal sounded crazy this time.

But the good-natured cop responded. "Yeah, yeah, I know hun'." He looked at me, "Nice to meet ya, Lady Vice President. Too bad you weren't here last week. Last week I arrested the Queen of England. Now, get going."

We spent the next several hours walking the streets of Cambridge. Eventually our group trailed off in different directions. Smaller numbers make it easier to find hiding spots. Finally, just Crystal, Ron and I remained. We sat on a stone wall and watched the sun come up. Ron turned to me and said, "Worst part of being homeless? You never get any rest."

PROVIDENCE, RHODE ISLAND

I'd bummed a ride from Maine to Massachusetts the day before, and now I awaited the arrival of another traveler to get me to Rhode Island. A guy named Matt gave me my first ride. He drove an extended cab foreign-made pickup truck. I threw my sleeping bag and clothes in the pickup body and hopped into the front seat.

The truck smelled a bit like wet dog... probably because of the pit bull that drooled and climbed all over me on the ride down. The dog was "fine, didn't hurt a soul, just kind of aggressive." I was, after all, in her seat.

What the heck? Free ride to Cambridge? Couldn't really complain about the arrangements. As the saying goes, "Beggars can't be choosers."

My hosts in Providence picked me up and delivered me by 10 a.m. A press conference in front of my childhood home had been planned for that morning.

My parents brought me home from the hospital to where we lived, the Chad Brown housing project. The G.I. Bill and affordable housing had made it possible for my "other side of the tracks" father to go to medical school.

The son of a Boston cop, my dad worked in the residency program at Rhode Island hospital when I came along. My folks already had three kids and couldn't afford much. One of my dad's favorite stories to tell is about one of his interviews for medical school.

He went to Boston University, but applied to other medical programs as well. His story tells of the response from one of the other admissions officers who told my dad that education was a luxury a man with so many children couldn't afford. If it hadn't been for the Chad Brown housing project, they might have been right.

This trip around the country highlighting the poor necessitated a visit to the affordable housing unit that had made my family's climb out of poverty possible.

When the press conference ended, I walked around the buildings of my old neighborhood. It looked more spacious than I recalled. And many of the features of the landscaping had changed. Our entourage of political supporters and local candidates made a bit of a scene as they flanked their fraying Vice Presidential candidate. As we passed an open doorway to one of the housing units, the family that had spilled out onto the walkway asked us why we had come.

There sat a grandma, some adult children and a few grandkids. The grandma greeted us warmly. When she learned that I had lived there at one time and that I was now running for Vice President she got very excited.

A Vice Presidential candidate, a product of Chad Brown? She said that she just couldn't believe it. She wanted to know everything. How old had I been? How old was I now? Did I say 262 Chad Brown St.? Why, that was right around the corner. She would take me there. She got up stiffly and pointed around the corner to my old home.

She looked up at my face and beamed as she said, "We were neighbors, you know?"

I asked her, "Really, where did you live?"

She replied exuberantly, "Where I live right now! Right around the corner."

She further elaborated, "In fact I'm only two years older than you. I bet we played together."

She had lived in that same housing unit since 1958. She had children and grandchildren there. She had never moved away, so she never needed to move back. Nor did she think that she would ever leave. I met her children and grandchildren. She introduced me as though I had been that absent prodigal who finally returned.

And she told me that she wished more than anything that her long-lost neighbor from 262 Chad Brown St. would become Vice President.

We moved away when my dad finished his residency program. Even though 41 years had passed, I had the most vivid memory left over from living there, and now as I stood with her I wondered if I had daydreamed it.

So I asked the grandma if she remembered giant sandboxes. "Oh goodness, you remember those sandboxes? I loved those sandboxes too. We were all so sad when they took them out. Six or eight or 10 of us could play in one of those at once. Bury someone up to their neck in them, just like at the beach."

She finished her explanation with a forlorn look on her face. "They took them out 'cause they got dangerous. People started leaving stuff kids shouldn't play with in them and people were getting in trouble. So they took them out." Then she glanced around and pointed around the grounds and said, "They took a whole lot of the buildings down too. Made it less crowded. Don't you think it looks less crowded?"

I responded that I had noticed that right off, that it looked much more spacious. But I wondered, with less housing available, if my father had been in college today, would he have been able to find a place for us to live?

ROGER WILLIAMS PARK

Singer Michael Jackson in 1983 made a 14 minute video of his hit tune "Thriller." In it, a group of recently unearthed creatures clothed in rags, with distant looks on their faces, march up an alley en masse and eventually break out in song.

As I marched through downtown Providence, Rhode Island, with a surprisingly large number of homeless people toward the federal building we mirrored the imagery of that music video.

Our parade through the city drew stares from passersby; their faces looked as though they saw the same similarity to the ghoulish music video. People crossed the street to avoid our procession. Certainly it would have seemed appropriate had Vincent Price, the narrator in an interlude during the song, materialized chanting, "Creatures Crawl In Search Of Blood To Terrorize Y'awl's Neighbourhood."

The revulsion and avoidance that people exhibited during our procession indicated that this demonstration would successfully increase support of the area homeless -- if any support might be gained at all -- as a result of fear rather than empathy.

The number of participants in our demonstration in Rhode Island surprised even the most accomplished of organizers. The disaffected aren't known for banding together. Activists in the area had succeeded in bringing dozens of marginalized individuals out to rally on the front steps of the federal building.

The large turnout resulted in part from the dedicated efforts of our supporters in the area -- folks like Richard Walton, who has long struggled for political change but has also spent decades working with homeless men in Providence. Richard knew how to contact the affected persons, and those folks themselves had decided to take a stand. Many voiced concern that their already bad situation was getting worse.

The president of the United States, in conjunction with Congress, instituted a moratorium on Section 8 housing. This federal subsidy program, paid to landlords, defrays some of the rental cost for low-income people and assures a place for them to live. Some of the banners and signs held by participants in the march proclaimed that the administration had gone in the wrong direction for affordable housing. Other signs simply demanded understanding and change.

On the edges of our march, to one side or the other, fights periodically erupted. If you've seen video of lava flows, where the center of the flow is just molten rock, but the edges of the flow come in contact with other material, trees or houses and those start burning, that was what this human flow did. The simmering tempers weren't any cooler in the middle: they just didn't ignite until they got to the edge of the group and in contact with other elements.

Sometimes onlookers shouted vulgar comments; often the male marchers returned those in kind. A handful of the participants fell to the back of the pack and had shoving matches.

"Creatures Crawl In Search Of Blood To Terrorize Y'awl's Neighbourhood."

As the gathering stood on the steps to the federal building a gentleman from the United States Attorney's Office approached and said that they had no record of a permit for any event and that the protest would have to disperse or relocate.

While the gentleman remained at all times polite, he drew some venomous responses from the protesters.

"We will one day have to rise up and fight this government," proclaimed one of the more vocal attendees.

The gentleman just reminded him that he had no permit to hold a protest at the federal building and that he needed to leave.

We proceeded to the park where the Rhode Island organizers had planned for us to spend the night.

In 1635, Roger Williams was banished from the Plymouth Colony in Massachusetts for espousing religious freedom and democracy He fled west, settling in what would become the state of Rhode Island. Our search for a safe place to sleep, brought us to Roger Williams National Park.

A lovely green space, just a couple of city blocks in size and in the center of Providence, marked the place where Roger Williams had found a fresh water spring.

When we arrived we pitched the tents and anyone who wanted to sleep in them could. The tents weren't just for the organizers or me; in fact most of the organizers went home to sleep. This was an opportunity for the local indigent population to have a little fun camping.

When we asked what the local homeless needed – so that we could provide it as part of our ongoing attempt to leave the folks in the are where we stayed better off than we had found them – we were told that they wanted to have a regular night like everyday folks do.

The federal government has jurisdiction over Roger Williams Park and the local authorities cannot enforce vagrancy laws there, so many homeless folk sleep there when they have nowhere else to go. Consequently, the volunteers for the campaign decided on a camp out and to avoid the added complexities of cooking, we had a pizza party. Local supporters brought tents for all of us to use. They collected money and bought enough pizza for any and all homeless folks who wanted to eat. Volunteers continued delivering pizza for hours.

The local organizers had struck a deal with the Citizen's Bank office building to use the lobby restroom. Recently built, it had marble and glass and brass fixtures. The doors of the bank were not flung open to us freely; a doorman greeted us on our way in and out of the building. The uniformed, well-spoken gentleman who monitored our visits to the bank spoke with me cordially and meekly, but only after I spoke with him first. He had been told that a Vice Presidential candidate would be sleeping in the park with some homeless folks and would need to use the bathroom. He had no idea which of us it was, and because my name was "Pat," he had assumed that it was a man.

After I introduced myself, and we made small talk about how Providence had changed since I lived there, he volunteered his opinion of poverty in the United States.

He explained that folks like him didn't particularly dislike the folks that lived in the streets. He explained that they just didn't want to get too close to them.

I stood there wondering what this doorman made for a salary. Nice bank, nice uniform, handsome, clean, all his teeth. Maybe $10 or $12 an hour, I imagined. Maybe married, maybe two incomes, maybe an occasional tip that paid for his bus fare.

As I wondered this, he said, "The problem with people like me living on the edge is, it means if you go to pull somebody else back up, they might actually pull you down."

Richard Walton walked me back to the park. We talked about self-preservation as a motivation for inaction, and as we approached the park, two women began screaming.

"Creatures Crawl In Search Of Blood To Terrorize Y'awl's Neighbourhood."

One of the women had fallen asleep. The second woman had used a razor blade to cut her. By the time we got back to the park, other folks had broken up the fight. The cutter had moved on and the first woman came to talk with me.

She hated her life. Mental illness infected everyone after a while. If you weren't crazy when you got to the street, living there made you crazy. No wonder they took that crazy bitch's kids away. Things had to change. Couldn't I fix it?

The Providence police pulled up next to the park during the night. They shone their bright surveillance lights from across the lawn at our tents. They couldn't come on the park property, but they could keep an eye on us.

Because of the park, my trip to Providence allowed me to spend the night with a group I really didn't see gathered in one place again for the rest of the trip. Nowhere else, would I spend the night with the angry, intoxicated, mentally ill stereotypical homeless again: Only where Roger Williams' memorial to religious freedom offered these folks a freedom of their own.

The Providence police pulled up next to the park during the night. They shone their bright surveillance lights from across the lawn at our tents. They couldn't come on the park property, but they could keep an eye on us.

Because of the park, my trip to Providence allowed me to spend the night with a group I really didn't see gathered in one place again for the rest of the trip. Nowhere else would I spend the night with the angry, intoxicated, mentally ill stereotypical homeless again. Only where Roger Williams' memorial to religious freedom offered these folks a freedom of their own.

THE MODEL

Campaign volunteer, Cynthia, brought me to her home on the way to the train station. I took my dirty belongings into her house. I had wanted to leave them on the doorstep but she wouldn't let me. She told me I had some extra time left between leaving the park and catching the train. She had put clean sheets on her bed and told me after my shower I could nap.

The shower was hot and the water pressure strong. It took me awhile to get all the clothing layers off: being naked felt strangely vulnerable and out of place. Sleep deprivation or dozens of startling moments or some combination of the two made me feel like something would happen at any minute that would necessitate me being dressed.

I used her shampoo and soap to wash. When I got out of the shower I noticed that she had laid out lotions and other toiletries. I moisturized my face, my arms, my chest, my legs: my skin felt so dry. The cold damp nights made me feel brittle. I considered briefly but determinedly about putting the lotions into my bag. Shaking my head at the sudden urge for kleptomania, I left the bathroom.

As I left the bathroom she met me in the hall with fresh fruit and yogurt. The sweetness and wetness of this breakfast seemed new and delightful. Cynthia looked past me at the toiletries on the counter. She said, "Oh, take those, I bought them for you."

Her gifts made me so happy. I scurried back into the bathroom, still clutching my breakfast bowl and tossed the little tubes into my bag. While planning for the trip, I hadn't thought about such niceties being necessities. I had no idea that such small comforts would become so valuable.

Cynthia's bed, soft and warm and filled with pillows, smelled so clean. I smelled so clean. I fell asleep for an hour and a half. I woke up and dressed and with a feeling of great resignation got into her car. She drove me to the Providence train station.

On the way a reporter from Maine Public Broadcasting called to interview me, to get an update for the folks back home about my experiences on the homeless tour so far.

In passing she mentioned that she had pitched the story to National Public Broadcasting. She said that she hoped that they would pick up her stories as she followed me around the country.

The national Associated Press had picked up on the notion that a Vice Presidential candidate was snaking through the country and done a quick print story. But other than local media, no news organizations thought it news worthy.

Almost exactly one year to the day later, as hurricane Katrina battered away all the barricades that blind the media to the conditions of the poor in the United States, discussions of poverty would become vogue. But it was still 2004 and that discussion just hadn't hit the Presidential race.

Inside the train station, I called our campaign press person, Blair Bobier. I spoke with him virtually every day. He maintained the blog on our website that chronicled my journey. I asked him for the number for National Public Broadcasting. He got it for me, along with the name of the contact who assigned stories and I called the man.

I went immediately to his voice mail. I left my name and phone number and a brief description of why I had called. Then I shouldered my bag and made my way toward the train.

A new high-speed train had started running along the Northeastern corridor. I had a ticket on the most modern passenger train in the United States. I would be in New York City in a matter of hours.

The train was luxurious. Clean and bright and roomy, the new high-speed accommodations impressed me. I put my gear up over my head and sat down next to a beautiful African-American model coming back from a photo shoot in Boston. The model smiled politely at me. I silently thanked Cynthia that I didn't smell bad anymore.

An hour into the trip, my phone rang. The gentleman from NPR identified himself. We discussed my reasons for taking the trip, that my desires to highlight different issues in the campaign motivated the journey. He voiced a passing interest in maybe catching up with me later on as the trip progressed.

Media is like that. Starting an arduous task isn't news: but finishing one sure could be. He couldn't make any promises, but he might do something at the end. (Or in the middle if I got stabbed to death, I thought). We finished our polite goodbyes and I hung up the phone.

The model reached over and took my hand.

I'm so proud to sit next to you. But, you can't sleep in the streets of New York City. I couldn't help but hear your phone call with that reporter. I'm sorry to butt in... Are you all alone? You can't be doing this all alone. I'm going to give you my phone number. You can call me night or day. I will come and get you; I'll send a cab for you. New York is an awful place to be alone and poor. Before I got this big contract in Boston I had to live with somebody that took me in just because I was pretty. Oh please don't stay in the street. Please, just pretend, and then come stay with me. You'll get arrested, if not worse. You know that don't you?

I acknowledged the kind offer and voiced my appreciation. I finally had to promise that I would call if I got scared and I took the phone number.

We moved on to a discussion about modeling.

The train sped our way to New York as I learned that models

had to settle for a good paying gig, that there were just too many beautiful people who would never make it to the big time. Every model had to find that niche that would give them a chance to work, to use their talents, to pay the bills.

Long arms, long legs, beautiful face and quite busty considering the slight frame, my new friend was a lingerie model. Staying in great hotels, posing for three or four days a month, this model could pay every bill and then some. (There was certainly enough money to rescue me with a cab!)

I asked to if there were any shots from the current shoot. There were.

As the pictures were shown to me, as erotically posed and revealing as they were, I learned something new about my beautiful companion. This highly paid provocateur had a scrotum and a penis.

As a young man I was lost and had no purpose. Now I have a home and a job and friends. I'm a beautiful woman and I surround myself with people who know the value of what I do. I'm safe when I'm at work. I'm respected and pampered and treated like I matter. I travel and eat in great restaurants and I'm allowed to talk about love lives and kissing and I never wear sensible shoes. Beauty and vulnerability are respectable. Ugliness and weakness are not.

How many heterosexual men had bought her a drink? How many had held the door for her? How many would be angry to know that she wasn't what she appeared to be?

The irony of running a campaign of substance in the shadow of a campaign of image sat embodied in the beautiful creature next to me. Unable to be the man society accepted, she had become the manifestation of society's desires.

NEW YORK CITY

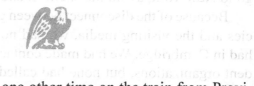

The cell phone rang one other time on the train from Providence to New York City. The director of a not-for-profit group, Picture the Homeless, called to say that the authorities had contacted him regarding my visit to the city.

During the process of setting up the tour throughout the country, the campaign staff had been notified that no member of the press, or political candidate was welcome in shelters of the Big Apple. In fact, we were notified that if we attempted to stay in any of the shelters, we would be arrested.

What could possibly be so special about homelessness in New York City, that secrecy was justified? There were image problems associated with New York, but did that warrant threats of incarcerating politicos and members of the media?

Did conditions in the shelters warrant the risk of more bad press for the cops?

The police in New York had gotten their share of bad publicity. The Republican National Convention and the coincidental protests had resulted in thousands of arrests and hundreds of charges of brutality.

Earlier in the summer, a NYPD police officer had been suspended for not arresting a homeless man. The papers reported that the officer defended his decision by explaining that the homeless fellow hadn't bothered anybody or done anything wrong.

But in New York, the law says that sleeping in the streets is wrong.

The campaign committee agreed that New York could not be left out of our Left Out Tour. In New York on the night that I stayed there, more than 37,000 other folks had nowhere to go. A population the size of many U.S. cities could not be ignored. We decided to show solidarity for the police officer who placed his job at risk, and risk getting arrested ourselves. We decided to go to New York, avoid the shelters, and sleep in a public park.

Because of the disconnect between government shelter agencies and the visiting media, we had no homeless escorts as we had in Cambridge. We had made contact with different independent organizations, but none had called us back. Compounding the situation, the unfriendly climate toward the homeless population in the nation's largest city had deteriorated even further in the midst of the election year.

Both the Democratic convention in Boston and the Republican convention in New York City had resulted in the displacement of thousands of homeless folks from their usual surroundings and routines. Health clinics in Boston within the vicinity of the Fleet Center had been closed, and access to the general delivery post office used by the transients of New York had been cut off to them.

No medicine and no mail. Homeless folks who lived in the Madison Square Garden area had been collected and relocated. Anyone who attempted to return to 'their' side of the barricade got arrested. For those delegates attending the political convention that would build a platform by which our nation would be run, no homeless person, no panhandler, no vagrant was visible to remind them of their plight.

When I answered the phone, the director for Picture the Homeless said, "I just got a call from the authorities. They said that you are coming to New York City to live as a homeless person. They told us that if you gained access to a shelter that they were going to have you arrested and prosecuted. They called me cause they thought maybe you would contact us for help."

I responded that I had contacted Picture the Homeless for help, but that his organization hadn't gotten back to me.

He said, "I know. I didn't call you back because I didn't think we could help you. But the authorities just notified me that if any of us help you that they aren't going to just arrest you. They said they would arrest us too."

I attempted to interrupt him and say that it had never been my intention to cause any trouble for the homeless communities and that I completely understood and would just sleep in the park.

He pressed on telling me that if there was that much concern about what my presence could do, that he had to help me. If the authorities thought that I could make that much of a difference, then maybe I could. That making a difference was what Picture the Homeless was all about, and that they sure needed some sort of difference made in the city of New York.

He gave me directions to his office.

I got off the train at Penn Station and made my way the 70 or so blocks uptown to find him, hoping I wouldn't get arrested. I had a train to catch the next day for Washington, D.C., and it was a Friday night. Would a bailiff be available on a Friday night? And how quickly would my staff be able to post bail?

I responded that I had contacted Picture the Homeless for help, but that his organization hadn't gotten back to me.

He said, "I know, I didn't call you back because I didn't think we could help you. But the authorities just notified me that if any of us help you that they aren't going to just arrest you. They said they would arrest us too."

I attempted to interrupt him and say that it had never been my intention to cause any trouble for the homeless communities and that I completely understood and would just sleep in the park.

He pressed on telling me that if there was that much concern about what my presence could do, that he had to help me. If the authorities thought that I could make that much of a difference, then maybe I could. That making a difference was what Picture the Homeless was all about, and that they sure needed some sort of difference made in the city of New York.

He gave me directions to his office.

I got off the train at Penn Station and made my way the 70 or so blocks uptown to find him, hoping I wouldn't get arrested. I had a train to catch the next day for Washington, D.C., and it was a Friday night. Would a bail it be available on a Friday night? And how quickly would my staff be able to post bail.

JACKIE & GENE

How could the Island of Manhattan, which was purchased in 1626 for only $24, be so darn big? It took a long time to get from Penn Station to 116th Street. But meeting Jackie and Gene, my homeless escorts, made the trip worthwhile.

When I first arrived at the office, we watched videos that Picture the Homeless had made depicting the living conditions of thousands of people. Via videotape we witnessed the displacement of area homeless residents during the Republican convention. While this video highlighted the 'don't see, don't deal' approach of many governmental agencies, we also saw videos depicting the systemic problem of residence-less-ness that exacerbates the homeless situation.

Shot after shot displayed the glut of available empty buildings around the city. We discussed the numerous vacant buildings all over Manhattan and the reasons that they stayed vacant, rather than becoming affordable housing. The folks at Picture the Homeless said that when one building goes empty it waits idly for the others on the block to follow suit. Vacant buildings have a tendency – especially as they become more run down and as they become havens for drug activity or other illegal behavior – to become contagious to the adjacent buildings.

Once a block becomes vacant it is prime real estate again: to a developer. The city or the state or some federal agency stepping in and reclaiming one decaying building in a still in tact block 'messes with the capitalist food chain.' Why have an urban high rise of affordable housing units, when the whole block can give way to development?

The Picture the Homeless folks told me that it's all about the landlords. "There's only one thing more powerful than a politician in New York City, and that's a landlord," explained Gene, who would be one of my companions for the evening. He continued, "Even in the shelters, it's about the landlords. It isn't that the city doesn't pay money to house homeless people, it's just that they get in with the property owners and then no one cares how the homeless get treated. It's quite a racket. Take as much money as you can to care for or house the homeless, put out as little as you can, and pocket the difference. If you own the politicians, you can keep doing this forever."

The shelters harbor every kind of danger. Most homeless folks don't want to go to them. But it's against the law to be out on the street, so folks have to go. The landlords own the politicians, the government pays a per-resident dollar amount to house the homeless, the politicians pass laws that force people into the shelters or incarcerates them, the landlords get rich and buy more politicians.

After a few lessons on how the government agencies providing social services work, we were ready to set out for the evening. The Picture the Homeless staff had a plan. The director gave Gene and Jackie $20 to take care of me. We would wander the streets of New York City until curfew time, and then Jackie would take me into a woman's shelter and Gene would leave us there.

I shouldered my bag and out we went.

New York Italians, and those who love them, were celebrating St. Gennaro, the patron Saint of Naples. The St. Gennaro festival, complete with delicious food, music, dancing, and street acts filled New York's Little Italy.

Food, drink, and trinket vendors crowded the sidewalks. We moved through the streets in a cumbersome fashion. Gene walked especially quickly and I had trouble staying up with

him. I would bump into folks and turn to say "excuse me."
Gene, a veteran of these streets, passed fluidly through the
crowd. We walked boldly through sidewalk cafés, squeezing
between diners.

On the tables sat pretty cocktails and gorgeous meals. Patrons dressed in their casual finest glanced at our little vagrant
train as we moved between them. Some folks had expressions
of dismay that we had the nerve to walk through the café. Others looked away as though we were offensive, or simply weren't
there at all.

When we got to the other side of the festival, Gene asked
if I was hungry. I replied that I was starving and the delightful
smells coming from the sausage vendors had pushed my hunger over the edge. "Good," he smiled, "I wanted sausage too."
He turned to Jackie, saying, "you want sausage too Jackie?" It
was unanimous.

I took my money out of my pocket. I had my credit card
and license in the same pocket. Gene looked at me horrified.
"Is that how you carry your important stuff? You must want to
get robbed!"

He pulled a little black pouch from a string around his neck.
"When we are done here, we are going to get you one of these.
You let it hang around your neck, inside your clothes, if some-
one touches that, you will feel it!"

"And besides, this is my treat." He said this with such a look
of pride that the finest writer in the world couldn't duplicate it
with words. "We were told to take care of you, even got money
for it, and that's what we are doing. Tonight, you are in our city
and you are our guest."

Jackie smiled at me too. She lacked Gene's boisterous nature. In its place she had a sweet stillness. She told me to let
them show me the fun side of their world. I would see the part
of their lives where they moved seamlessly from one end of the
city to another; seldom noticed yet witnesses to every kind of
life. She explained that the diversity they could show me was
imaginable only in a city with tens of millions people.

We got our sandwiches and went over by the band. Gene found a plastic cup on the ground. It was a festive commemorative cup with the date on it. Still in fine condition, the owner had carelessly discarded it after finishing its contents. Gene gave it to me and proclaimed that we even had souvenirs of the event.

He asked me to hold his sausage sandwich for a moment and ran up the street a few storefronts. He returned with two beers each in a small brown bag. "Jackie doesn't like beer," he told me. He handed me one and said to keep it in the bag or we'd get in trouble.

I thought of the sidewalk cafés we had walked through, with the pretty drinks and open beer bottles on the tables and wondered how the distinction was made between the public drinking that was legal, and other types that were not.

We stood a few hundred feet from the band. They played music from the '50s and '60s and Gene danced around in our space. We devoured the delicious sandwiches and drank our 'hobo beers' and waylaid a little longer. Finally my cheerful hosts announced that we had a schedule to keep and needed to keep going.

I mused about what would happen to our rags if we didn't get in by midnight. We had become reverse Cinderellas still needing to leave the dance in time, but with a different set of consequences if we returned late.

On our way to the shelter on 7th street we took many detours. We went to Chinatown and I purchased a small black pouch like the one Gene had so that I could keep my valuables close to me, especially while sleeping.

Then we traveled to SoHo where Jackie desperately wanted to show me something.

There seemed to be no stars in the sky, making the night very dark. I had lost track of where we walked blocks before we got to SoHo. Gene and Jackie told me stories and I stared at their faces far more than at the landmarks around me. I asked them about 9/11 and where they were when the planes hit.

Gene got really agitated as he spoke. He had been *couch surfing* at a nephew's house.

Couch surfing was the most universal bit of homeless lingo that I encountered on my travels. Each community had its own set of slang terms and often they didn't correspond to similar terms in other locales. But couch surfing meant 'finding someone with a house who'd tolerate you a few nights to get you off the street' and it meant that every place I went.

Gene's grand-nephew woke him up and told him to look at the TV. Gene looked at what he was watching and told him that he shouldn't look at violent movies like that; that there was already too much violence in the world. The boy replied that it was real and it had just happened.

The nephew lived up in the 120th blocks. Gene ran all the way down to 14th Street, as far as anyone could go. He told me that by the time he got to the lower end of Manhattan he had started seeing some of his friends that lived in the area of the Twin Towers. But at the time he told me the story, he still hadn't found four of them. He figured they had died when the towers collapsed. No one could tell him for sure.

Gene said that his four friends had lived there for years, in the shadow of those towers, but because they were homeless, the authorities couldn't list them as residents and so Gene had no way to verify their existence.

If they didn't register in the list of dead at the Twin Towers it was because no one ever validated that they had lived there. And Gene felt that the official attitude was one of complete indifference. If living there didn't matter, how could dying there count?

Jackie pressed onward toward a restaurant she wanted to show me. She spoke of Alsaltian French food and what great meals these restaurants of SoHo served.

Then we stood in front of a trendy place with dark wood paneling and fantastically alluring lighting. Jackie and I had our faces pressed up against the glass looking in at the bar. She pointed to the far bar stool and told me that she wanted me to remember this place and come back when this trip ended.

She told me that I should sit on that stool and order a martini and make sure that I had pretty clothes on and my makeup done just right. Jackie told me that Robert De Niro came to this restaurant all the time. She said that many times she had peered in the window at him and watched him drink or eat or talk to pretty women.

Jackie said that she could tell that dressed up I would really get his attention. That he would talk to me and learn that I had a gorgeous heart as well as a pretty face and he would help me. She got very excited explaining that Robert De Niro would discover me and then I could afford to move to New York and live near her and that we would be friends.

I asked her if she would come with me and we could eat Alsaltian food together.

She said not when I came to meet Robert De Niro, but afterwards she would come. After her plan had worked and I had been discovered, then we could come together for dinner.

We turned away from the window. Gene waited patiently for us on the street. We had peered in the window talking for 10 or 15 minutes. Surprisingly, no one had shooed us away from the building. As I turned and looked at the entryway to the restaurant, I saw many patrons walk in and out the door. No one asked us to leave, because no one noticed us at all.

Gene ushered us toward our destination at the shelter around the corner from Madison Square Garden. Along the way he met a friend of his, a young African-American man with a grocery store carriage full of returnable bottles.

They exchanged pleasantries and then introduced us. The young man was Gene's business partner. Gene explained that together he and the young fellow collected thousands upon thousands of bottles and cans a month. Gene wanted to make a video of their work and send it to Budweiser. He said that Budweiser drinkers littered the most.

Gene further explained that if it weren't for him and his partner, the nice folks in New York City would know what irresponsible people these Budweiser drinkers were and that impression would negatively impact the brewery. Because he and his buddy picked up the discarded bottles and cans the truth about these patrons stayed hidden.

Consequently, Gene felt that the company, for having these guys protecting their corporate image, should compensate them. Once Gene sent in the video, he was certain that Budweiser would agree.

Gene said the role of the homeless would probably never be valued; that it was a sin not to see the value in even the lowliest of people.

I stared at the carriage full of empty beer and soda bottles and wondered what the real death toll in the World Trade Center was, when you counted Gene's lowliest of people.

sible people these Budweiser drinkers were and that impression would negatively impact the brewery. Because he and his buddy picked up the discarded bottles and cans the truth about these patrons stayed hidden.

Consequently, Gene felt that the company, for having these guys protecting their corporate image, should compensate them. Once Gene sent in the video, he was certain that Budweiser would agree.

Gene said the role of the homeless would probably never be valued; that it was a sin not to see the value in even the lowliest of people.

I stared at the carriage full of empty beer and soda bottles and wondered what the real death toll in the World Trade Center was, when you counted Gene's lowliest of people.

BAG OF BAGS

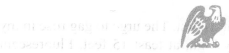

We turned the corner onto 7th Street and Gene told us he didn't want to leave. But, smiling sadly, he reminded us that he couldn't go into the women's shelter. I didn't want him to leave either. He made me feel safe and he told me so many fascinating things. His ideas were novel and comical and tragic. I could've talked to him all night.

We might have chosen a co-ed shelter, but with the threat of arrest hanging over our heads, we had to pick a shelter that didn't demand identification. Most shelters do demand ID and if you fear discovery, you simply can't stay in them.

I hugged Gene goodbye. Gene, probably 70 years old, was thin: all muscle and bone. His clothes had made his body seem more full. His black face, his gray hair, his full-face grin that lacked a number of teeth made him look like anybody's grand-father. How many other grandfathers lived on the street?

Jackie and I turned to go into the shelter. All the good humor of the night vanished as Gene walked away and we walked into the building. Jackie grabbed my wrist and sternly cautioned me, "Do exactly what I tell you to, and don't look anyone in the eye."

Earlier in the evening Jackie had been collecting loose paper from bathrooms and left-over plastic bags. She had a plastic bag that contained them all. She would crumple the papers up and stuff them in the bag and didn't seem to have anything else in there but bags and paper.

I had watched her do this all night. I dismissed the behavior, assuming that the woman who wanted me to knock Robert De Niro off his feet might have been a little eccentric. What the heck, just some paper toweling and plastic bags. No harm, no foul.

She clutched this bag tightly as we waited in the entryway. She told me to keep my sack close, especially because mine had my sleeping bag and clothes in it. I didn't look at anyone's face but I scanned the room.

The smell in the room hit us first. The urge to gag rose in my throat. The ceiling was very high, at least 15 feet. Fluorescent lights that hung from the ceiling lit the room like an operating theater. A woman sat behind the desk, processing folks as they came into the shelter. Four or five women stood in line ahead of us. We waited our turn.

Jackie took advantage of the wait to give me a few pointers. "Don't take the blankets, they're usually infested. And don't take your sleeping bag out. It'll get bugs too. Don't breathe too close to anyone. They're sick." She pointed out the tuberculosis machines that hung from the walls around us.

Another woman in line with us added to Jackie's comments. "They're always sick here," she said.

The smell was making me sick. Not only would I take their advice and not breathe close to anyone, I tried very hard not to breathe deeply. I looked against one wall and I saw a woman with a bandanna folded in half and tied around her face like a Wild West outlaw. I wished that I had one of those, just to cut the smell, although I would've bet that she wore it because of the germs.

The room, approximately 15 feet by 30 feet had about 80 women in metal and plastic chairs. The chairs reminded me of middle school lunchroom chairs. Not very large, and sculpted molded plastic that turned the corner where your butt sat. Two television sets hung from the walls. At first I thought that this was the waiting room; that we would move upstairs at bedtime.

But there was no upstairs, no beds, just chairs, infested blankets and stench. Upon closer inspection I realized that many of the women had already fallen asleep.

Just before we got checked in, paramedics from St. Vincent's came to help a woman who appeared very sick. They took her past us on a stretcher. Ghastly sight, ghastly smell. I thought of the AIDS statistics I had learned in Boston. I wondered what kind of saints worked at St. Vincent's.

Jackie told me that she would go first. She had to identify herself, but I must give a fake name. Jackie, while brave enough to chance bucking the authorities, didn't want to get arrested either. I used the name "Jackie Price." She told me to tell them that I had lost my identification and when asked why I came there for shelter, to say that my husband beat me and I had to flee.

I am the world's worst liar. I hate to lie. I handled the missing ID and the fake name pretty well, but when she asked how I came to stay there, I choked. I looked at my feet and I honestly felt like I would faint. The smell, the sick woman, the coldness of the room, I felt my senses fleeing. Just as I thought I had blown it, the woman behind the counter said in a rough voice. "Never mind, I understand. You know you can only stay here one night, maybe two, without ID. After that we have to turn you away. You need to find a domestic violence shelter after this. They take the people like you."

Of course! I looked like I would faint; I must've looked scared. She instantly assumed that I was one of the tens of thousands of women fleeing an abuser. She asked me if I wanted a blanket. Following orders, I said that I didn't.

Jackie and I walked halfway down the room. The temperature was about 50 degrees. They kept the room cold because it reduced the transfer of disease. The blankets would keep you warm if you dared to use them. We did not.

We set down across from a woman who had already fallen asleep. Jackie explained that her posture, leaning back with her head hanging over the back of the chair made her vulnerable to both assault and falling from the chair.

Jackie went on to tell me that she had her collection of bags and paper toweling so that she could hold it on her lap. It served as a pillow that you could afford to lose. If it got infested in one of the shelters or stolen: a few trips to a restroom and you'd have a new one made. If you held something on your lap and leaned forward over your legs, you had more stability to prevent you from falling, and you weren't so vulnerable to attack.

Jackie's apparent eccentricity was actually sheer practicality and resourcefulness.

I looked again at the woman across the way, the one splayed back in her chair. She looked like a depiction of Nefertiti, the African goddess. Her beautiful broad nose and brown face looked noble and serene as she slept. The goddess in the plastic chair gave off a noxious odor that made me keep my hand over my face. I looked at her seemingly clean face and upper torso and wondered from where the smell came. Then I looked at her feet.

Nefertiti's swollen feet festered and reeked of infection. I grimaced at the thought of what pain such an infection might cause. African-American, 30-something woman with rotten flesh all over her feet. I diagnosed her as a diabetic. I have no medical credentials. I have no clue what gangrene smells like. Still, I was pretty certain of her condition. I thought of her great grandmother. I imagined the day that she might have been emancipated. I tried to imagine what freedom might feel like to a slave and how she might have wept for her great granddaughter's feet.

Jackie roused me from my thoughts. She told me to go and get a cup of hot water before they turned the lights down. She told me to get two and she would watch my stuff. I told her I didn't want hot water. She said to get it anyway.

I walked back, winding between the women sleeping or trying to sleep in their chairs and affirming in my mind that I would die of thirst before I would drink anything from this room. When I got back to Jackie she told me that the water wasn't for drinking, it was for holding – that the hot water would keep our hands warm in the cold room.

Survivor Jackie, plastic bag Jackie, hot cup Jackie, all the super-heroes in the comic books didn't have her resourcefulness. We whispered to each other through the night. Hearing Jackie's voice soothed me and helped me tolerate the place. Jackie told me about her own fall from security and regular life. Her husband had died and shortly thereafter she had gotten cancer. Her illness used up all of her resources and she had to sell her house to pay her bills.

In her late 60s she lived a marginal life, but was still getting by when she had her heart attack. This more recent illness had pushed her over the edge and she hadn't made it back since. There she sat, bent over her plastic bag pillow, a 71-year-old woman with beautiful white hair done up in a bun and a severely tattered sweater telling me her story. Also bent over, listening, I stared at her cloth shoes lined with paper towels to keep her feet warm.

She didn't usually come to this shelter; she could usually go to one of the other ones if there was room. Tonight she took me there to maintain anonymity, this shelter of last resort. It was full because at the end of the month all the shelters filled up with folks whose checks run out before the month does.

I wanted to leave. I'd had enough. Walking back from a bathroom that I wished I had never seen, I stepped over several different kinds of insects. When the fluorescents lit the room, the little critters stayed hidden. Once those big lights went out, they roamed the floor freely.

Upon my return to our chairs I told Jackie that I wanted to leave. I announced that I had definitely seen enough. "I've got some money" I said. "Let's go ride the subway the rest of the night."

Jackie said that we couldn't go. We'd get in trouble. We had to stay for services.

Services? This shelter didn't have a religious sponsor; I didn't understand. And anyway, it was Saturday morning. Did they have services every day?

She told me that I could get away with missing services, that I wasn't coming back. But if she missed services too many times she would lose access to all of the shelters.

The stench nauseated me and my skin crawled with psycho-somatic illness and a fear of bugs. I stayed about another hour watching the second hand of the large wall clock go around. Jackie dozed off as I stayed beside her one minute at a time. I managed by promising myself that I would only stay one more minute, and if I could stand that minute, I might try and stay another one.

The hardest night of my life was the night my mother died. Except for that, no other night has ever been more difficult than staying there so that Jackie wouldn't get in trouble for missing services.

At 3:44 a.m. Jackie woke up and looked over at me. "You can't take it any more can you?" she asked. I said that I really didn't think that I could. I told her that I kept trying but I didn't know how much longer I could stand the sound of the coughs, the odor of the people, my anxiety at the thought of closing my eyes, any of it.

She got up and selflessly said, "Let's go ride the subway."

Outside, I had Jackie explain why "services" were so impor-tant to her. She explained that it was all part of the process ... the racket that the politicians and landlords have going. Finally, I announced that I didn't know what praying had to do with land-lords.

Complete understanding came to Jackie's face. We spoke a different language and now she could translate. The "servic-es" weren't religious. Anyone who stayed in a shelter and ever wanted to return had to participate in "social services." Before you left you had to meet with social workers or therapists or both. Every resident who ever wanted to return had to be evalu-ated, every time.

Folks like her and Gene, who were just poor and had nowhere to live, had to keep getting evaluated. She agreed that occasion-ally there were a few mentally or psychologically impaired folks who needed these services, but for all the rest it was just a money-making deal for somebody doing business with the government.

Instead of putting Jackie or Gene through evaluation after evaluation, why didn't they just fund affordable housing so that they could get out of the system and off the street?

I looked down and thought maybe a pair of little old lady shoes would be a good way to spend the money as well.

HOPPING THE TRAIN

The island of Manhattan has more than 100 McDonald's restaurants on it. And that's just one fast-food chain! It is inconceivable that all of those low-wage earners have homes in the vicinity of their employer. All those low-wage jobs: 37,000 homeless New Yorkers: makes perfect sense.

After spending several hours riding underground in the Big Apple, Jackie and I made our way to Penn Station. I had a train to catch to Washington, D.C., and I wanted to buy her some breakfast. We went into the McDonald's in the station. I thought of asking the woman who waited on us where she lived, but decided against it.

I tried to give Jackie some money. She wouldn't take it. I asked for her mailing address so that I could stay in touch. She told me that I could write to her in care of Picture the Homeless, that they would know how to get it to her. Then a flicker of trust ran across her face and she gave me her general delivery address. She said that it would be a good way to find out if her mail got through on a regular basis.

When she gave me the information, I realized that neither of us had used our real names all night.

Strangely, it surprised me that she had lied to me. But of course, one could never be too careful.

We finished eating, I picked up my ticket at the ticket counter and Jackie walked me down to the train landing. When the train pulled up we both got on and took seats. This remarkably clever woman suddenly took on an absent-minded attitude, as though she wasn't sure whether or not she belonged with me on the train.

As the train pulled away from the station she had a sparkle in her eye.

Who cares about rules and regulations in a world where the laws of decency had long ago been abandoned? What did she have to lose by being caught on a train without a ticket? No jail could be worse than that shelter. Why couldn't she have what she wanted on this train ride, just a little taste of rebellion?

One small victory in the face of so many battles lost.

The conductor came through and asked for our tickets. Jackie looked at him blankly and said that she had come on to wait with me and when the train had started up she was too scared to step off of it. She looked at him as if to say, "How could this harmless little old white lady have purposely done anything wrong?" He told her he'd come back with a return voucher so that she could get back to the city. She thanked him very sweetly.

When the conductor finished securing her return trip, Jackie looked at me and said, "I wish you had her power."

Stymied again by my little homeless escort, I had no idea what she meant.

She continued, "I wish you had her power: I wish she was you. Then she would help us. If she had come to talk to us: She promised to come talk to us. Instead she sent a tape."

She could tell that I still didn't understand. She sighed, "I wish you were Hillary."

Instant clarity: Hillary Clinton: Super Jackie's United States Senator. By now she had stepped off the train and onto the landing. I apologized for not being Hillary Clinton. Jackie was right; Hillary could've helped her.

Jackie tried to explain the reality of her life. Jackie said that Hillary could help the homeless but that she doesn't care, and that I cared but I couldn't help.

I walked back to my seat and collapsed onto my bag. I pulled out my notebook and wrote furiously the words that Jackie had said. I put the pen down and fell asleep.

I woke up what seemed like seconds later, as the train pulled into Washington, D.C.

WASHINGTON, D.C.

I stood in the Community for Creative Non-Violence building, also known as the "Mitch Snyder House." This 1,350-bed facility housed men, women, and children. One entire wing of the facility housed homeless veterans.

Mitch Snyder, some folks say the nation's most famous homeless advocate, had himself served time in Vietnam.

His notoriety began in the 1980's when he led hunger strikes to raise awareness of the homeless situation in the United States Capital. He staged public funerals for homeless people who froze to death on the streets of Washington D.C. Across the street from the White House he built "Reaganville," a tent community for the poor.

Snyder demanded shelters for the homeless as well as affordable housing. He completed three hunger strikes in all, the last one demanding the money President Reagan had promised to renovate an old federal building. The money would provide the upgrades necessary to transform the office building into a shelter.

During his last hunger strike, Snyder had nothing but water to drink for nearly two months. His impending, avoidable death, in 1984, an election year, put great pressure on the Reagan administration.

Finally, Ronald Regan relented. And on the night before what ended up being re-election day for the 40th President, Reagan guaranteed Snyder the money.

Our workers on the ground in D.C. had arranged a tour for me of the facility that this money created.

Several administrators of the shelter greeted me as I stood there, in the lobby of the house where Mitch Snyder lived and ultimately died by suicide. We went up to the main meeting room and they spoke with me at great length about what it meant to them to be a part of the shelter.

The men who spoke had more in common with Mitch Snyder than just caring about the homeless. Like Snyder they had all done time in jail.

Just a few years before Mitch founded the shelter, he had three square meals and a roof over his head in Danbury, Connecticut, at the federal penitentiary.

One of my hosts served time in a segregated cell because of his penchant for violent behavior. He used the knowledge that he had to overcome his own violent past to help other homeless folks who showed up for shelter. He knew what it felt like to be filled with anger and lack the tools necessary to deal with that anger.

They were all men of great faith. Snyder had learned about faith from the Berrigan Brothers. Daniel and Philip Berrigan, famous for peace action and civil disobedience, had served time with him at the federal pen. My hosts that day also shared Mitch's religious fervor. They believed that the right amount of faith could cure any man.

As we sat and chatted the shelter directors made me aware of the rules. These rules were pretty simple. Nobody visiting CCNV should judge folks by their past AND no politician should even think of coming to CCNV for a photo opportunity. These men made the point quite clear, that they would no longer be exploited.

They told me that George W. Bush had come to the shelter not long after his inauguration. Initially they were elated to have the President put them on his list of priorities. But when he arrived their hopes met with disappointment.

The President arrived at CCNV with his usual compliment of Secret Service agents. He had a pan of paint and a roller and he rolled some paint on one of the walls in the very room in which we sat. His entourage took a bunch of pictures and then they whisked him away again. He didn't listen to the important things that my hosts had wanted to tell him and Bush's rapid departure had left them all disillusioned.

The large contingent of security seemed to wound their pride the most. It offended them that they were not trusted to safe guard the President while he visited the shelter. Worse still, because the Secret Service came in the room with them where they had hoped to be heard by the President, it appeared that the President's security detail believed that one of them might actually harm Mr. Bush in some way.

They vowed not to be used for political gain like that again.

I looked at the three supporters who had picked me up at the train and brought me to the shelter. Not a Secret Service agent among them. And while they had no guns to thwart would-be attackers, Asa, one of the local volunteers, did have a pocket full of peanut-butter-and-jelly sandwiches that his wife had made to protect me from hunger.

One of my companions, Jay, spoke up and told our hosts that he certainly didn't accompany me as any form of protection. He identified himself as one of the local supporters of my campaign. And as important as my being there might be, because he lived in D.C., he would still be there, working in the community, long after I had moved on to my next shelter. He merely wanted to learn what they had to teach.

With that out of the way, apparently satisfied with our sincerity, these powerful passionate handsome African-American men began to speak.

One man in particular mesmerized us. His entire body bent and twisted as he wrung the descriptions of their lives out of his own thoughts. As he spoke of drugs and alcohol, anger and violence, poverty and ignorance, his body became covered in sweat. He described the 12-step programs and outreach services available at CCNV.

He wrung out the difficulty of housing rapists and rape victims in the same building. He painted pictures of "gestational, cultural, and situational pain."

Substance abuse: sure it was a problem, but with the other things these folks had lived through, was anyone really surprised that many of the street people were users?

As I watched his body language and listed to his words, it struck me that he performed a very elaborate and often rehearsed dance. As though all the words he needed to say were printed one at a time on different blood vessels or ribbons of muscle. This speech never written on paper, instead etched inside him, ran its course through his body as he spoke. Each blood vessel waited its turn to deliver the next perfect thought or word to his brain so that he could speak them.

How moved might George W. Bush have been if he had stayed to hear this man's story?

Statistically, CCNV staggered the imagination. They had never had a paid staff person. Housing 1,200 to 1,700 individuals a night, CCNV had employed 92,000 volunteers in its two decades of operation.

And each and every night since the shelter opened its doors, several hundred United States military veterans slept there. Each of the veterans who stayed there, trained to kill or die for their homeland, ended up with no home of their own.

As I left the shelter one of the men said that he had been surprised by my interest in poverty issues. He thought that my political party was just about the environment. He said that he would learn more about it because a political party about the planet was a waste of time. Because our group seemed to care about the economy and people and not just trees he would rethink his opinion of us. He told me, "The earth don't need us, we need us."

THE HOLY SEE

The Vice President of the United States lives in the Naval Observatory, which is located on Massachusetts Avenue in the United States Capital. Congress designated the home for the Vice President in 1974. Prior to that, the second in command just lived in his own home. Keeping those homes safe became costly to the U.S. taxpayer and Congress decided to provide housing to spare further expense.

Ironically, the first Vice President to actually live in the mansion was Ronald Reagan's right-hand man, George Herbert Walker Bush. While Mitch Snyder wrangled with President Reagan to provide housing for the thousands of D.C. residents with no where to go, George and Barbara Bush busily unpacked their belongings and moved into their housing paid for by the people.

The night that we stayed there, the shelters in D.C. had the same overcrowded conditions that Boston, Providence, and New York had. So we opted to once again sleep in the street. Although this time we picked the Vice President's Street.

The neighborhood is filled with embassies. Directly across from the Naval Observatory sets the Vatican Embassy, aka the Apostolic Nunciature, the Holy See. And just a few blocks away stands the largest church in the United States of America, the National Shrine of the Immaculate Conception.

We notified the D.C. authorities that we intended to sleep on the ground in front of the Church of Rome, facing the house of the Vice President. The people of D.C. own the side walks, the people of the United States own the Naval Observatory and the Pope had our backs. Our request to sleep there was honored.

We had invited the folks from CCNV to join us that night. While many voiced an interest in sleeping out under the stars with us, the distance between the downtown shelter and where the ambassadors sleep is quite great.

While the shelter residents didn't make it, dozens of campaign supporters came to spend the night. Folks drove in from Virginia and Maryland. We sat on the sidewalk for hours holding signs that invited Vice President Cheney to join us. Unfortunately, he never came.

Many of the Vice President's neighbors came by though and took the time to speak with us. Those who chatted with us didn't particularly like their neighbor in the observatory. It wasn't political; they were sick of all the construction. We sat there and watched for hours as enormous trucks hauled huge steel girders through the front gate of the compound.

Following the September 11th attacks on New York City and Washington D.C., Congress had approved the building of an eight-story underground bunker beneath our national historic landmark, The Naval Observatory. We were told that since the scheme began an endless parade of heavy construction vehicles, a cacophony of blasts and explosions and a continual rain of silt and soot accompanied the project.

One of the neighbors had nothing to contribute but questions: "An eight-story underground bunker? For what? What was this administration planning? And why were they the only ones who were going to live through it?"

I had a different question: How much affordable housing could you build for the price of an eight story underground bunker? If Mr. Cheney had come to greet us, we could have asked him.

Shortly before dusk the authorities of the Holy See crossed their beautifully manicured front lawn and came to speak to us.

The police had posted round-the-clock sentries that stood about 30 yards away. And though their mission was probably to protect property and not to protect us, I felt quite secure. The Secret Service had their eye on us as well, so the Vice President certainly had nothing to fear. Whether or not the neighborhood felt comfortable with us sleeping there, it seemed we would learn momentarily.

As the gentlemen in long black robes with beautiful crimson piping and Roman collars approached us, I stood to greet them.

I introduced myself, and they seemed well aware of our project. They had come outside to tell us that we needn't sleep on the sidewalk. The representative who did all the talking offered us the softness of the Papal lawn. He stressed that we couldn't approach the house in any way, but that he felt it quite unnecessary that we lay on the hard unforgiving ground in the presence of the stewards of forgiveness: even though it completely broke protocol to let us on their property.

While this small kindness sounds like a small kindness, the difference between a concrete sidewalk and three inches of plush manicured lawn defies understanding by anyone not in the situation. And though the representatives of the Church of Rome sent to interact with the government of the United States didn't particularly like the idea of us getting near their doors and windows, they helped make our vigil more comfortable.

We moved our sleeping bags off the sidewalk and onto the Vatican Lawn. Once safely tucked inside my bed, exhaustion overtook me and I fell asleep. I slept more soundly than I ever have, before or since.

Asa, whose wonderful wife had made us peanut-butter-and-jelly sandwiches, woke me the next morning and said that an independent media group from New York City had called. They had heard too late that I had been in New York and they had gotten in their cars to drive to D.C. and interview me before I left for Tennessee. He told me to get into his car and he would take me to his house so that I could get cleaned up for the interview before he drove me to Dulles International Airport for my flight.

Ron in Boston was right: The hardest thing about being homeless is you just don't get any rest.

I shook the sleep from my head and stuffed my sleeping bag into my travel sack. About half of our crew lay sleeping near me; the other half sat off to the side whispering in the early morning hours. The volunteers had taken turns staying awake and keeping the rest of us safe. It seemed unnecessary, with all the police that the city and federal government had hired for the night.

Such is the paranoia, justified or otherwise, of sleeping in the street.

FAX MACHINE

The film crew took us off schedule. They had gotten down to D.C. from New York City as fast as they could. They shot digital video for about an hour and, with still many more of their questions unanswered, we left them for the airport. They expressed a desire to meet up with me in some of the other cities on the tour. They wondered if they could interview me again. I said that I was flattered by their attention and that I'd do whatever I could to get spread the stories of the homeless people that I encountered.

Asa drove as quickly as he could to Dulles airport. While still in the car I pulled my license from the little black pouch I had been wearing around my neck since New York and raced to the airline check-in counter. E-tickets made getting a ticket easier, but travelers still must show identification. After leaving the automated screen with my ticket and my license in hand, I was screened by the desk attendant and ran for my gate.

My carry-on bag, also known as "last night's bed," in one hand and my ticket and license in the other, I made a very quick side stop to the restroom. Then, with very little time to spare, I ran to the security-check area. As I prepared to hand my license and the boarding pass to the TSA screener I realized my license was gone.

With only a very few minutes to spare I retraced my steps through the ladies room and back to the check-in counter. I asked the TSA attendants for help. I assumed that they would be alarmed in this time of terrorism fear that a valid driver's license might be laying on the floor of one of the nation's most congested airports.

The TSA folks blithely informed me that I didn't need to notify them of the lost license, although they cordially wished me luck finding it.

I ran down the stairs to the information desk where a line of visitors to the nation's capital were ahead of me waiting to find a good hotel or check on arrival times of shuttles. I waited impatiently. I jiggled my leg as the anxiety of misplacing my ID mixed with the aggravation I felt at myself for losing it in the first place. Finally, with mere minutes to spare before my flight would begin boarding, the very nice woman behind the counter turned her attention to me.

No one had turned in a license. She would keep watch for one. No, there was no way to use the public address system to ask if anyone had found a license. Sure, I could give her my cell phone number and she would call me if she found it.

I walked away, headed toward the clock on the wall that had stopped clicking off the minutes to my boarding time and had begun clicking off the minutes to my plane taxiing down the runway and leaving without me.

I hauled out one of my "not really homeless" indicators, my cell phone, and I called Tracey, my personal assistant back home.

Tracey stayed in my house while I was away and took care of my kids. She took care of my personal life. She cooked meals. She ran errands. She straightened my life out so that the few days a month I managed to spend at home were devoted exclusively to my family. And now she was called upon to fix this mess too.

I asked Tracey to look in the alcove to the left side of the stove hood and see if she could find my passport. She did and she could. At home I live in a small town with a Main Street full of friendly merchants most of whom had fax machines. One of the merchants was also a family friend and Tracey called her to see if she would open up (it was Sunday morning) and let her in to use the fax. She would and she did.

While Tracey made these phone calls I raced back to the information desk to see if they had a fax machine that I could use. They didn't. I raced to the TSA folks to ask the same question. They had a fax machine but I couldn't use it. I tried the airline. They didn't have one, but they assured me that they would have let me use their fax machine if they only had one.

Tracey called me back. She was in the business on Main Street with my passport in her hand ready to fax a copy as soon as I gave her the number. I stood on the upper level of Dulles airport, recently reassigned to a flight that it didn't appear I would be able to make, clutching the cell phone and staring at the bank kiosk right in the center of the room. I told Tracey to give me a minute. I had one last resort to try.

I walked up to the bank teller and explained that I needed a very important fax. I asked her if I could get something sent to her fax machine. She glanced over her shoulder at the fax machine behind her, looked back at me and said, "I don't see why not."

If not for the several inches of safety glass between us, I would have kissed that girl.

She passed a piece of paper with the number on it through the slot at the bottom of the glass and within minutes I stood in line holding the faxed photocopy of my passport.

I wondered if a faxed photocopy was a valid ID. I steeled myself for the worst and handed it to the attendant with my boarding pass.

VICE PRESIDENT OF WHAT?

I sat on a plane next to a big, robust, burly white man. He wore an open collar shirt, casual slacks and a gold signet ring. About 40 years old, this guy affably started up a conversation with me the way he likely did with every person he met on a plane or in an airport lounge.

I sat there completely harried. My belongings stowed in the overhead bin, my notebook and pen on the tray table in front of me, my seat belt fastened and never so grateful in my life to be on a plane experiencing bad turbulence.

I hate to fly and I happily accepted the opportunity to talk to this cheery fellow and have him take my mind off the choppy air that had engulfed our plane.

Reminding me more and more of the John Candy character in the movie "Planes, Trains, and Automobiles," this traveling salesman told me a little about his life and then asked me why I made the trip from Washington, D.C., to Knoxville, Tennessee.

Too tired to delete the important yet hard to explain details, I told him the naked truth. I was running for Vice President. Yes, of the United States of America. And, ready for the kicker? That I was living in homeless shelters around the country.

He looked, not surprisingly, baffled. When he found his thoughts he asked me, "Does this mean you don't like George Bush?"

Now, I must have looked baffled. Stymied that this part of my full disclosure seemed to be the only thing of interest to him, I sighed, "No, I don't like George Bush."

He turned away from me, looked out the window, and didn't speak to me again.

When the plane landed, I let him out of his window seat before I took my bag down from the overhead compartment. He glared at me and left.

—

KNOXVILLE, TENNESSEE

We stood in the public square in downtown Knoxville collecting bed sheets for the YWCA transitional housing facility. We gathered around the table as volunteers gradually stacked dozens of sets of twin bed sheets on the card table that we had put there for the event.

Once the display was taken down and the donations delivered to the YWCA, several of the Knoxville-area supporters took me down to the day shelter to greet folks. Dozens of homeless people stood along the outside wall of the building. My escorts had brought voter registration forms. We spoke with approximately 50 shelter guests and registered 11 to vote.

A pretty young woman with short brown hair and a cute little nose stayed with us nearly the whole time. She identified herself as "Pixie," and while the name definitely described her appearance, my recent experiences made me doubt the authenticity of her name.

Pixie had a seemingly limitless comprehension of politics and current events. She said that she spent most mornings in the library reading newspapers and surfing the Internet.

She told me that in addition to being pretty savvy when it came to politics, there wasn't anything she didn't know about the mental health "racket" and the way it gets used to manipulate homeless people as well as taxpayers. She wanted to bring me up to speed on the systems and how they worked.

I explained to her that my days in these shelter situations went by too quickly and that other people planned my schedule. I didn't feel that I could process her entire repertoire of knowledge on the street, but if she gave me her e-mail address, I would write and learn from her all this detailed information that she was trying to share.

She refused.

As we walked off, Pixie asked where I would be staying later. She made me promise that I wouldn't stay in this one particular shelter that she said was dangerous and filthy. When I told her I'd be staying at the YWCA transitional housing facility, she said that I would be OK there.

Then Pixie walked away.

Over at the YWCA, the management staff had allowed our Tennessee supporters to hang posters and say that I would be spending the night. They gave us the meeting room on the first floor and our Knoxville crowd had set up a cookies-and-coffee event that evening for all the residents who wanted to come and meet with me.

About 15 women came down from their rooms for the meeting. We talked about how they ended up being homeless and how the residents came to live in this transitional housing. Most of them had been on the waiting list for months.

All of them had come from the streets – though none of them had started out there. Many had left behind horrible marriages when living in the street proved preferable to living in the marriage.

Two of the men we had met over at the day center dropped by as well. They told us of the marginal lives that they were leading and that most of the area shelters couldn't compare with the YWCA for cleanliness or opportunity.

In the back of the room stood a tall, striking African-American police officer. I thought that she had come to provide security for the event. She hadn't. She had come because she used to live in a shelter herself. She wanted to meet the female Vice Presidential candidate who actually thought living with the homeless made sense. She had come, on behalf of every homeless kid that she had known growing up, every homeless kid who probably would never make it out the way that she had, to say "thank you" to me for trying.

The rest of the group listened to her with profound interest. They voiced dismay that she had been able to do so much with her life after being a homeless young woman. She said she pinches herself over it every day too. I thanked her for being with us. Her presence gave hope to others.

Because the local desire, in addition to getting new bed sheets, of this group was learning more about voting, our Knoxville supporters brought voter registration cards. Those in attendance were told, as had been everyone at the day shelter, that it didn't matter what political party they joined, or if they joined one at all.

Several of the women had never registered to vote. Some women had registered years before but had moved or let their registration lapse. They asked many questions about history and current events. They asked about politics and politicians. I answered their questions the best I could but told them to read the paper and go to the library.

I told them that as a voter they could make a difference. I also told them that they had to ask their own conscience what was the right way to vote.

The evening went on for hours. The residents told their stories. Most of the women worked in low-wage jobs and the YWCA made it possible for them to save apartment down payments and security deposits.

The woman who worked at the front desk in the lobby had asked us to prop the door open so that she could hear our discussion. Eventually, she dragged her desk over to the entryway so that she might contribute as well.

When everyone finished talking and the cookies were all gone, the street folks who had dropped by went back out to the street and the residents went upstairs to their rooms.

I had a very nice room, adjacent to a clean bathroom. Each of the accommodations was either a single or a double. Compared to the last few nights, I felt like I was staying at the Ritz Carlton. These women seemed to feel as fortunate as I was feeling to be in the YWCA transitional housing facility and not asleep on the street or worse.

When I spoke to the police officer after the meeting broke up I asked her what could possibly be wrong with Knoxville if they had a facility like this one. She answered that what was wrong with Knoxville was that they didn't have five more facilities like this one.

The waiting list for this facility hovered around 18 months. I got to stay there because the woman whose room I used voluntarily bunked in with someone else for the night.

As I left the great room to head upstairs to the bed and toilet and shower that would be mine for the night I noticed someone standing off to the side of the lobby. It was Pixie, the homeless sprite from outside the day shelter. She came over to me and handed me a note with her e-mail address on it.

I told her that I would write. She said that she would too. Pixie and I are still writing to each other. I follow her progress and worry about her when she disappears from e-mail for a month or so.

The police officer and I write to each other too. She uses her real name, and isn't afraid of getting in trouble. Consequently, I've been able to interview her on the radio and discuss issues like getting educated and on your feet from America's most vulnerable position: youthful homelessness.

It took a year to figure out what Pixie had left to do during those several hours between meeting her and her returning with her contact information.

She had walked to the library and signed up for a new e-mail address. One with the fake name she had invented for the lady that claimed to be running for Vice President. Then she had walked back downtown and gave it to me. One can never be too careful.

RUSTY BOX

   I went upstairs to a small bare room with just a few indicators of individuality in it. There was an alarm clock and a couple of cosmetic items. Some instant soup mix and granola bars. The bathroom had a wonderful hot shower, so I took one and got into bed.

   Sleeping in a bed in Knoxville, with sheets and blankets and a desk upon which I could put my wallet and my notebook and not worry about losing them, gave me the opportunity to do something I hadn't done all week. I had a dream.

   Several years earlier my children and I accompanied a busload of school kids on a trip from Maine called the Heritage Tour. I went as a broadcaster to chronicle the trip for the parents, sponsors and listeners back home. It had been hosted by a subsidiary of the YMCA in Waterville, so maybe it's the YWCA/YMCA connection that made me dream about it.

   On the tour we went to Philadelphia, Gettysburg, Washington, D.C., and New York City. One of the tour's features included a trip to the tenements in New York where the immigrants settled after arriving in the United States from other countries. We went to the Tenement Museum and then a tour guide brought us upstairs to show us one of the tiny little apartments where entire families of eight or more people would live in just one small room.

   They showed us the rusty coin boxes where the residents deposited coins to activate the gas for the stove or the heater. They had nearly rusted through as the shivering tenement dwellers mastered the art of carving ice slivers into the shape of nickels and dropping them in the box to keep from freezing when they had no money.

In my dream, I stood under the rusty box that hung from the kitchen wall. I looked past the clothesline hanging as a room divider to where the tenement's one bed stood. Behind me the sink overflowed with dishes mixed with laundry and the stove had tripe and bacon fat sizzling and popping as it cooked.

Propped up on the bed with a coverlet of worn quilted squares and a collection of rumpled plastic bags as a pillow sat Jackie, my little old lady guide from the New York City homeless group. Her sore and swollen feet were propped up in front of her on another makeshift pillow.

In the dream Jackie looked at me and said, "You remember being here with your kids? You remember the tour guide telling you how the poor would suffer together as families in these tenements, taking turns sleeping, taking turns working different shifts during the day, cheating the gas company, doing anything they could to survive? Then she told you that these tenements aren't like this any more. Families don't suffer together in poverty like that any more."

Dream Jackie leaned forward from her reclined position on the bed and continued, "This poverty, these horrible conditions, they aren't over. They're just restyled. Families don't suffer together any more; strangers suffer together now."

I heard someone doing the laundry/dishes behind me and I turned away from Jackie to see who it was. Standing between the sink and the stove, tending the tripe and washing the dishes with a drenched tuxedo jacket as his washcloth, was the old man from Cambridge who had nearly been beaten by the young punks. He stopped and stared at me for a moment and then resumed his dish chore.

I woke up in a room, safely locked and ever so quiet. The dream made me afraid that I'd never stop thinking about this trip.

I wondered if the day would come when I might sleep without dreaming of this trip? In my mind I hoped that these experiences would not haunt my nights; in my gut I was ashamed of myself for feeling that way.

FAYETTEVILLE, ARKANSAS

In late September, 2004 hurricane season built to a crescendo. With no direct flight available between Knoxville, Tennessee, and Fayetteville, Arkansas, my plane was first bound for Atlanta, Georgia.

As we approached Atlanta, so, too, did Hurricane Jean. The small jet with four seats across and about 15 rows back didn't just rock to and fro and back and forth. At times it seemed to twist at an angle away from its proper direction. Finally it landed and we disembarked the plane, one harried group of travelers. We relaxed a bit in Atlanta, as the nation braced itself for a regional upheaval similar to the one experienced by the individual homeless across the country every day.

The airport in Fayetteville, Arkansas services the Wal-Mart corporation. Once my connecting flight pulled up to the gateway, I walked into the terminal that paid tribute to the Walton family. Mrs. Walton had been a big supporter of air travel and the airport was named after her.

We initially picked the Fayetteville area because of the Wal-Mart connection. We wanted to see what kind of homeless shelter stood in the shadow of the world's largest employer. Lawsuits have since been fought and won by states who fault Wal-Mart's poor pay and employment practices for an increase in the state's need for public assistance programs. Maryland has led the way in passing legislation requiring the retail, grocery, and shipping giant to pay its own way.

We had a great deal of trouble getting a shelter to accept us in the Bentonville/Fayetteville area. Finally, I made a few phone calls and pulled some strings I still had left from my broadcasting days.

In Maine, as a radio morning show host, I had worked extensively with the local Salvation Army. I called the Major of a local unit and told him that we needed him to interceded on our behalf with a Salvation Army chapter down south. He made the necessary phone calls and vouched for us. Fayetteville's Salvation Army director called me himself.

The director told us that he didn't think we would want to stay there if we knew what it was like. He told us that their food bank cupboards were bare and that the outlook for it improving was bleak.

He said that they lacked local support and the economy had fallen off so badly in the area that he didn't think he'd have anything to offer us except more homeless people than he had the food, beverages, or toiletries to maintain.

We told him that we appreciated his willingness to let us stay. We told him the day and time that we would arrive, and then we got to work. Our in-state media coordinator for Maine, Derek Mitchell, got on the phone with every radio station in the Fayetteville area. He booked me on morning shows a week or two in advance of our visit and wrote public service announcements about the dire conditions at the food bank and the adjacent shelter. We officially put out the call for help.

Then our volunteers on the ground gut to work, speaking to individuals and local merchants and organizing food drives. When we pulled into the parking lot of the Salvation Army that day, we brought many pickup truck loads of food and necessities. A local television news crew was there and we all helped unload the donations.

The director of the shelter stood virtually speechless. He looked at me as we stood together in his now almost full warehouse and said, "Who are you people and where did you come from?"

I told him that while I came from pretty far away, the rest of these folks were his neighbors. Once the introductions were through, our Arkansas supporters said that he should call them if he ever got in trouble again.

My supporters left, and the director and I walked over to the shelter building. I walked in to get processed and spend the night. The television reporter and the local newspaper reporter asked if they could come in with me. The Salvation Army director said that they could as long as they got permission from the residents before they took any pictures.

This shelter had that kind of clean smell with a dirty one underneath it. Very nice and excited staff members greeted us. Because of the enormous outpouring of necessities for the shelter we, for one very brief part of this trip, got the treatment afforded celebrities.

A visibly nervous young woman sat down with me at the end of the intake room to ask me the same questions she had to ask everyone before they could stay in the shelter.

At first she apologized for putting me through it, but I explained to her that understanding this process was part of the reason I traveled to her facility.

I answered everything truthfully. My name, last known address, any phone number where I might be reached, and then she asked me for my religion.

All the other questions were understandably mandatory if you wanted to stay there. Even though most people might have bristled at the idea of giving friend's or family member's phone numbers, they complied, because the necessity might arise to locate a guest once they had left the shelter.

But requiring a person to disclose their religion didn't seem necessary. I asked her if I had to answer the question and tell her my religion. She said that I did.

I said that I just believed in doing good things for the sake of goodness itself.

She wrote down Christian.

The media and I then walked into the women's dorm where I would be spending the night. At this particular shelter they had a women's dorm and a men's dorm. They separated married couples and made them stay in their same sex dorm.

The room I walked into had a series of bunk beds, with enough sleeping space for 10 or maybe 12 women. They had an empty cot on the bottom of the center bunk where I tossed my sleeping bag.

A beautiful woman with long blonde hair well dressed and about 35 years old sat in a chair near what had become my bed. It seemed as though she had waited there all day. Filled with excitement, she announced that she couldn't wait for me to get there and that she believed God had sent me to her. Then she thanked me for being His messenger.

I told the woman that I'd be right with her and finished up with the press. As the newspaper reporter went to leave she gave me her name and phone number and asked me to stay in touch or to call her if I needed anything. She looked like she didn't want to leave. I took Yvette's information and promised to call her if anything seemed pressing.

The next day, she sounded as surprised as I felt when I called her for help.

CRAZY DREAMS

During the intake process they warned me about a rash of contact strep infections that had swept through the shelter. After I washed up and brushed my teeth, I practically bathed in the hand sanitizer I brought with me.

Once I got my sleeping bag unrolled, I crawled into it. Our dorm room had women in every bed. Some of the beds had babies in with their moms. Arkansas was one of the states that took children away from homeless parents – but only after they have finished nursing. The sound of suckling babies went on all night. Some of the moms told me that they kept nursing their babies longer than they preferred to so that the state wouldn't take them away.

Our dorm room had women – ages 18 to about 40. I don't know if other dorm rooms had older women or if this room was just for women with children. None of the other rooms' occupants ever came into the room and we weren't allowed in their rooms.

The women all started telling their stories. Most of the stories involved children.

The pretty blonde told me that she had been dreaming about George Bush. I asked her if she meant the President or his father. She meant the President.

And although not personally in her dreams, his dad figured into them prominently too. In her dreams, W sat waiting for his dad to come sit with him in the family limousine, a little boy all alone waiting for his dad.

Having recently started to have my own crazy dreams, I empathized to some degree with her and listened to the details of her imaginings.

She went on that God told her that George W. Bush didn't care about her. God said to her that it wasn't just her; that Bush didn't care about the homeless in general.

She got no argument from me.

But as her dreams went on, God explained to her that He would touch Bush's heart. That He would touch it and turn it toward His people. God would send her a sign and she would know that the time was near when the President would no longer look away from the poorest among them and he would "care."

When she heard that a Vice Presidential candidate would come to sleep in the shelter with her and the other homeless folks in little Fayetteville Arkansas, she knew that the time must be now. She knew that He had sent His sign.

I asked her to consider the possibility that it wouldn't be my visit that would turn the President's heart, but the election. I asked her if she thought it possible that George W. Bush would lose the election because he didn't "care" and that would drive home to him God's displeasure wth him for turning his back on the poorest among him. And then he would rethink his callous attitude toward the poor.

She said that she had never considered that possibility, but that she didn't think God worked that slowly.

Then sitting with the Bible across her lap, she explained to me how she came to be a resident at the Salvation Army shelter.

She had two daughters and, at one time, a husband. Her girls now lived in the state's custody because she couldn't provide them a home. She worked five days a week but visited them on the weekends.

Her husband had left them and she defaulted on her student loans. She and the kids barely made ends meet. This past April their precarious living situation looked like it would improve just in time to stave off homelessness because she had a large income tax refund coming.

Instead of receiving the refund, she received notification that the defaulted student loan payments as well as penalties and fees had dissolved her refund and she and the kids got nothing. A few months later, as they slipped further over the edge, their landlord evicted them and she came to the shelter for help.

Once at the shelter, the child protective services took her middle-school-aged daughters. She stayed at the shelter hoping to save enough money to get a place and reunite the family.

To further complicate the process of getting her feet back underneath her, shelter policy provided for no more than 30 consecutive nights' stay and then the shelter guests had to get out for at least 90 nights before they could come back. She only had a few nights left on this stay.

If the pretty little blonde was right and God liked to work fast, he really needed to get going for her sake.

A Native American woman in the corner bed said that she had just put her children up for adoption. She said that she didn't think the election would turn anyone's heart, certainly not hers. She said that as a convicted felon she had lost her right to vote so she couldn't change the system even if she knew how. She explained that her marginal living conditions meant that she went from having her kids to losing them to foster care every time she presented herself as homeless. She finally decided that she could love the kids best by giving them away to a more stable home.

I stared at the Bible in the blonde woman's lap. The Native American woman sounded like the Bible story about Solomon and the baby: she had sacrificed her custody of the children rather than figuratively cutting them in half. In Arkansas the government played the part in the story of the other woman who wanted the baby and didn't mind cutting it in half.

Right next to me, a very young woman lay in a bed filled with stuffed animals. Dozens of stuffed rabbits, cats, teddy bears, etc. crowded around her and threatened to fall from the bed. Probably about 20 years of age, this woman wanted to find a home and spread her toy friends all over her new place. She explained that while she felt cramped in her bed with all these creatures, she knew that one day they would all have a home.

She handed me a small stuffed chicken and told me she thought it would be nice for me to sleep with it there and then take it with me on the rest of my trip. She said that no one should have to sleep alone.

As the room started to quiet down, a woman who had slept facing away from us rolled over and began to speak. Quite a bit older than the other women in the room, she spoke in a raspy voice.

She told them all that they would never get homes. She had gone to see one that had been advertised in the local paper. The mobile home park on the rough part of town had several vacancies, and while she didn't really want to live there, she had begun to lose hope of ever finding a place. The homes didn't rent by the month, they cost anywhere from $110 to $160 per week. And while overpriced, these rentals were worth it because they made it possible to get your kids back.

At first the landlord greeted her warmly. She walked through a number of the homes and picked out the one she liked best. Back in the rental office she filled out the paperwork. After glancing at her application, her potential landlord asked her if she really lived at the Salvation Army homeless shelter. She assured him that she did.

The landlord then explained that he had made some sort of mistake. He just remembered that his partner had already rented the home she liked to someone else. He told her that he would contact her if anything else became available.

The woman said that the paper had said that there were several mobile homes available and she would take one of the others. The landlord replied that they had all been rented since that ad ran and he couldn't help her in any way.

She told the rest of the women in our dorm room that they'd never get a place no matter how much money they had. No one wanted to rent to someone from the shelter.

The next day, when my plane touched down in Denver, I pulled out my cell phone. I called the number from the ad and asked if there were any mobile homes available, the man on the other end of the line assured me that there were.

After hanging up from that phone call, I dialed another number. I called Yvette, the reporter whom I had met the day before from the local newspaper. I gave her the name of the mobile home park as well as the phone number. Then I told her the woman's story and her name and contact information.

Yvette asked me a few more questions about my trip around the country. She said that I sounded tired. I told her that the women and I had stayed up most of the night talking, but that I'd be fine.

Yvette asked me if I was going to be OK doing this homeless thing. I told her that I thought I would. Sometimes you just have to do what you have to do.

Then she excused herself from the phone call and said she had to go. Yvette closed by saying that she had to go see a man about renting a mobile home.

DID YOU GET YOUR CHORES DONE?

When I left Fayetteville, I had to leave quite early. On my way out the door this voice called out to me, "Did you get your chore done, Patricia?"

I said that I didn't know what chores I had to do. He showed me where to find the broom. Then he showed me the garbage bags. I looked at the clock on the wall – 5 a.m. I returned to my dorm room and changed the garbage. There were no rubber gloves available for changing the room's trash cans or the bathroom trash. All I could think about as I emptied the waste cans was the contact strep warning from the day before.

As I swept the lobby a very handsome man came up to me and asked about "the Vice President thing." He turned me toward the television in the lobby. CNN showed pictures of Hurricane Jean battering the southeastern United States.

He looked so familiar and as his wet eyes stared at me, I noticed that he looked like a brown version of the actor Tim Robbins. He launched into a diatribe of disbelief. "Look at how they react to a disaster. That's FEMA taking care of those people. Why? Because they are victims of a disaster. Why aren't we a disaster?"

Before I could tell him that I didn't know why, he pressed on with more details.

"I was the engine in my family. My wife volunteered and did nice things for other people but I was the engine that ran the house, you know? I owned my own company and we had plenty of money. I'm an electrician. I climbed up onto this exterior scaffolding one day and I fell. I broke my back. It's been more than a year and my insurance company still hasn't paid my bills. I've lost my home. I'm down to one car – the one we slept in until last night, when it got too cold to stay outside."

He repeated himself, "How come we're not a disaster?"

During his time in the hospital his wife had gotten a job, but she didn't really have any skills so the job didn't pay very well. They couldn't keep up with their payments.

"I'm the engine, not her," he said. "She didn't make enough money to take care of us."

And now he stood in the lobby of the shelter, watching FEMA respond to disasters, waiting for his wife to come out of the women's dormitory. No co-ed dorms in this shelter, they had to split up for the first time since they had lost their home.

When his wife came out they would leave. He had a bit of a plan. As a Native American he had tried to get help from the local tribe. Unfortunately for him, the local tribe wasn't Sioux. He had to find a Sioux tribe. So he and his wife would head west as soon as she woke up and they finished their chores.

I had just finished my chores so I wished him well. I had to head west too.

DENVER, COLORADO

A consortium of 12 multi-denominational churches had assumed the mission of combating homelessness in Denver, Colorado. Each church would adopt two to three families for one week at a time. The families moved from church to church until they got back on their feet. The family would then move into a more permanent environment, making room for another family to take their place in the revolving shelter program.

The homeless stayed in the respective meeting halls of each congregation. Office cubicle type temporary walls provided a minimum of privacy, while the volunteers who stayed with them day and night provided security.

Basically, the congregations learned about families at risk of homelessness by word of mouth. Most of them had small advertisements in their church bulletins and congregants or visitors alerted the staff about vulnerable families.

The night I stayed in Denver, a kindly soft-spoken older woman named Martha attended to our needs. One family, consisting of a mom, dad, brother, and three children aged 2 months through 7 years, kept mostly to themselves.

Martha said that in this environment shame was a pretty big factor. Most families had never been homeless before they came to this multi-denominational mission: To have a family retreat into their living space and not come out except for meals was rather common behavior.

The other family staying there that night, consisted of a mom and her two kids. They had fled domestic violence in California. The mom hadn't chosen Denver for any particular reason. She had to get away from her abuser and anywhere would do.

When the family first arrived, the mom thought that she had enough money for her and the kids to stay in a hotel until she found a job and could get settled. She hadn't realized that getting a good job with a hotel room as your home address was virtually impossible.

The mom couldn't say enough wonderful things about the mission. They had allowed her to use their street address and eventually get a post office box as well. She had landed a great job as an administrative assistant and would be moving with her children into an apartment shortly.

The mom and kids technically had never been homeless, and with the help of the mission, there was no reason to believe that they ever would be homeless. Although, according to the mom, if she hadn't gotten the call from a woman she had met at one of the other member churches, she and her kids had only two choices: go home to a horrible situation, or live in a shelter. She commented repeatedly how grateful she was for that call.

I liked the kids. They greeted me warmly and asked dozens of questions about history and presidents and what a person had to do to become a candidate for Vice President.

After we finished with our political discussion and their homework, we got out the playing cards.

The 12-ish son had long ago mastered the art of war: the card game of course. We played and laughed. Eventually, his sister went to bed, but we kept playing.

When his mom announced that he too had to go to bed, he came over to me and ceremoniously shook my hand. He asked me why I was so nice. I answered him, "Well, I guess because my mom was nice. She taught me to be nice. Just like you are nice and your mom is nice. I bet you learned to be nice someplace." But in my mind I thought about why he might have expected someone to be not nice. How un-nice had his home been?

How bad would life have to be to make a family journey into such an unknown and susceptible environment?

After both families had gone to sleep, Martha and I stayed up talking. Sometimes the residents needed to vent; other times the workers needed to vent.

~

Martha had a few problems with her government and her society that she wanted fixed. Earlier that month the computer system in the Colorado state offices had crashed. Consequently, food stamps and rent checks had not been issued in weeks.

She said that in her limited personal experience she had encountered many homeless and impoverished people with more than a passing knowledge of computers who could have been put to work correcting the problem. She told me that all food stamp recipients in Colorado had to do community service anyway, as a condition of their benefits. She wondered why the recipients could be used to clean up parks but not have their talents respected and employed to solve more pressing problems?

She further speculated that if no one existed in the indigent community with the expertise to correct the computer glitch, there unquestionably existed enough persons with the writing and math skills to process the checks manually.

Martha also had difficulty understanding how society could expect families to survive on low-wage jobs that lacked health care and other benefits? When families relied on social services because having jobs with substandard wages and benefits put their families at risk, her society criticized the family instead of criticizing itself for putting people so low on their list of priorities.

Martha had been volunteering to work with these families for years. She knew how much assistance people really got when they needed it most. And it sickened her.

"Remarkably," Martha added at the end of her discussion of the meager public assistance available, "very few of these people are grumpy. I think I've only met a handful of grumpy ones."

I told Martha, "I bet the grumpy ones have been homeless longer." I pointed to the sign cautioning about tuberculosis and added, "The most contagious thing I've run into in the shelters is anger."

Martha knew what I was talking about. She had some anger of her own.

SONOMA, CALIFORNIA

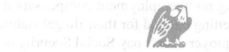

Nativo López, the national president of the Mexican-American Political Association, arranged to have me picked up at the airport.

Two of his representatives came and together we drove up to Sonoma Valley to meet the migrant farmers who worked in the vineyards. Arrangements were made for me to spend time with two types of alien workers – those who had come to the United States legally, and those who had not.

The entire Sonoma Valley, as far as we could see, shone in the beautiful sunlight. Our trip, several hundred miles long, took us through some of the most verdant rolling landscape I had ever seen. Scattered along the countryside we saw millions of grapevines and scores of brown-skinned folks tending to them.

According to my hosts, on average, vintners are the wealthiest farmers in the United States. According to the International Herald Tribune, California vintners are so profitable that they receive no subsidies. My MAPA guides echoed this statement and added that the average wine producer in California garnered a 300 percent profit on their investment.

The largest wine family in the United States, Gallo, bottles its wine using dozens of different labels – Turning Leaf, Andre, Ernest and Julio Gallo, to name a few. Because of the expanse of the Gallo Wine holdings, many of the migrants work for them.

While I met many migrant farmers, only about half of them were documented workers.

If a giant like Gallo or any of its smaller neighbors had anything to gain from hiring all these undocumented illegal workers, it had to be money. Undocumented workers are paid very poorly. Because the workers fear deportation, they don't complain about the bad wages or a lack of benefits. They can't complain to the authorities about having no unemployment compensation or no place to live without getting nabbed for their illegal status.

In addition, the employers don't pay Social Security or other related payroll expenses, nor do they concern themselves with the minimum wage. Workers in hiding don't complain about inadequate or nonexistent toilet facilities, water supplies, sanitation or first aid services.

Learning how the illegal workers were treated made a lie of the notion that vintners got no subsidies. The workers themselves subsidized the vintners that employed them.

My MAPA guides brought me deep into the woods to meet some of the aliens who sought shelter from the elements and the authorities often on the very property where they worked illegally. Tarps stretched between trees to shield them from sun and rain. Old car bench seats and abandoned mattresses served as beds and couches.

They cooked on open fires and used the wilderness as a toilet. The men I met in the woods had come from Mexico and all had families back home. One of the men hadn't seen his wife and kids in years. He faithfully sent money home every week, but didn't risk going back for fear he'd never make it over the border again.

They had a pan of beans and rice cooking on a fire. They offered to share their meal with us. We acknowledged their generosity, but confessed that we had dinner plans back in the town. One of the interpreters told me that there is an old Mexican saying, "If you have enough for one, then you have enough for two." I understood the sentiment. If you have enough food for one person to eat then you just eat a little less and share it with anyone who comes along. I looked into their small pan of beans and rice and decided the adage didn't apply in this case. It didn't appear that they had enough for one.

A reporter had come into the woods with us. He asked to take my picture with the men who lived under these conditions. I put my arms around two of them and turned toward the camera. The interpreter asked me to take another picture with my arm around the third man too. I obliged the youngest of these men and he thanked me.

The interpreter told me later that the young man didn't think just the married guys deserved a hug from the Feliz Vice Presidente.

We left the woods and went back to the legal migrant community. For the rest of the night my companions called me Feliz Vice Presidente, Happy Vice President.

Back in town a dozen or so legal farm workers put together a barbecue. We had a grand fiesta. They had marinated meat all day in spices and lime juice. They grilled it to perfection and then we ate it rolled up in flour tortillas. The barbecued meat had the finest flavor of any barbecue I had ever eaten. .

If only the men hiding in the woods could have had some this meat with their beans and rice. That would have made me the Feliz Vice Presidente.

THE FAMILY PET

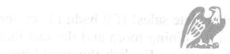

After the barbecue I went to the home of one of the resident aliens. He and his wife had emigrated from different parts of Central and Latin America. They met in the United States and fell in love. Her mom lived with them, as did her brother. They also had four children.

They had a simple home. Four adults and four children all under one roof, it would have seemed like a tight fit under normal circumstances. However, I felt relieved to be in a dwelling that had only nine people in it. The house had a kitchen, a dining room and a living room. The dining room had never had a dining room table. It had been turned into a bedroom for the grandmother and the uncle.

Upstairs they had three bedrooms. The boys all bunked in one of their rooms so that I could have the other. The opportunity to fall asleep as a homeless person had become a gift. Sleep helped make the lousy conditions go away. But when the surroundings included a bedroom with a door and a bathroom down the hall, it seemed a shame to go to sleep and miss out on the amenities.

The house, overcrowded by U.S. standards, contained very few furnishings. But it overflowed with camaraderie. While the mom and dad explained the difficulties they encountered getting property insurance and driver's licenses, the kids galloped around the house. The children's laughing outbursts didn't annoy the parents. Everyone in the house seemed happy that the kids smiled and laughed and played.

When I arrived at the breakfast table the next morning, the children sat clean and ready for school in front of their cereal bowls. Their school had sent the children home with chocolate sales forms to raise money for school supplies. They timidly asked me if I would be interested in purchasing some chocolate to help their school.

Fruit loops and school chocolate sales! If it hadn't been for the extra generation living in the dining room and the fact that the kids were the only ones speaking English this could have been fifth-generation White Middle America.

Why then did Middle America's talk radio stations attack the Latino immigrant population so vehemently? I would get a chance to broach that question later in the morning as a female talk radio host attacked my tour of America's impoverished areas and me along with it.

I bought chocolates from the boys and asked them to keep them when they came in and share them with their grandmother. They assured me that they would.

I turned to leave the house and stood staring slack-jawed out the window of the house. Outside the kitchen window stood a large extremely hairy animal. One of the children had a tether to take him/her for a walk. I looked by the kitchen door and saw a water bowl and a food bowl, like one would set out for a dog. But this was no dog!

I turned to another of the children and I asked, "Is that a sheep?"

He looked down at his feet and explained that it certainly was a sheep. It was their pet sheep. The young man explained that they had had the sheep since it was a baby. "A lamb," I said.

The boys had asked their dad for a pet. And while they had sincerely expected that they would get a dog, their dad had brought home the lamb. He continued to explain how cute and little their lamb had been. The whole family was happy and they bought food for it to eat, took it for walks, and let it in at night out of the elements to sleep with the family.

I mused with the boy that they had done the same for me.

By the time the lamb had grown to be a full-sized sheep they had all fallen in love with it and no one wanted give it up, so the parents had allowed them to keep it.

I asked if they had thought of shearing their sheep and making a sweater. The young man grew horrified. After some banter back and forth I realized that he thought I meant that they should skin the animal. When I explained the difference he calmed down.

He took me to show me the sheep's "pretty" face. And explained that it didn't have hair where it didn't need hair. I looked at its matted wool and decided that if the family, sheep included, liked things the way they had them, it wasn't my place to interfere.

We all said goodbye and I climbed into the van that would take me to the airport. Inside the van sat eight migrant workers who had ridden along to take me to my flight. They spoke very little English but they came anyway, to say "goodbye" and "thank you."

Our press people had arranged for an interview with a local talk radio station to coincide with my ride to the airport. I sat in the front seat with my cell phone and took the call when it came.

This woman launched into an attack of my tour of homeless shelters around the country. She accused me of wasting money on plane rides that could have gone to the homeless in the different states. She told me that if the homeless wanted homes, that they ought to get jobs.

All the morning's serenity and good feeling vanished. The camaraderie of the house I had just visited vaporized.

I told this caustic woman that most of the people I had encountered in shelters had jobs. I explained that responsible broadcasters would key into the fact that tax dollars got stolen by dishonorable landlords and funneled away from the intended recipients. I tried to show her that affordable housing could save government and society millions in other services and that there existed an additional moral imperative.

She called me a series of names: bleeding heart, fool, exploiter, attention-seeker and others. She told me that she felt comfortable speaking for the homeless and that they didn't want me interfering in their lives or living situations.

I said a corrupt system had allowed disreputable individuals to steal from the people of our country and that we needed to be able to expose the thieves. I said if I were a thief who came into her house she would call the police. I asked her why she didn't want to know if landlords or politicians were stealing from the taxpayer.

Then she told me that she hoped I broke into her house some day because she kept a loaded handgun next to her bed and that it would please her to no end to shoot me dead if I ever came in her house.

At that moment I knew that I had been infected with the number 1 contagion of homelessness: I didn't have a small dose; I had a full-blown infection. And I let loose with a fury I had never before felt.

I told her that she wouldn't speak for the homeless "on my watch." I shouted that I had seen a level of suffering that she clearly and unfortunately had never experienced. I exclaimed that a little dose of human suffering might cure her repugnant character, but that I seriously doubted it.

I gasped for air as I snapped at her that she didn't understand the nature of choices badly made for ulterior motives because she couldn't see that her radio station clearly had a secondary motivation when they hired her.

Her tone completely changed. She asked what I could possibly mean.

I said that the only reason to have a nasty reckless no-talent woman on the air was to have the voice of the oppressed do the bidding of the oppressors. I concluded by telling her that a woman putting down other women and minorities in their most vulnerable hours was the oldest tactic known to oppression.

The head gladiator, the senior trustee in the jail, the overseer in the field... they were all in place to keep their own kind down low.

I viscously spat out that she clearly didn't have the charm and grace necessary to do a real radio show and that she had sold her soul to those who would buy it so that they could secure their own elevated station in life. And that they laughed at her when she wasn't around to hear it! Then I hung up the phone.

When I did everyone in the van applauded. Only two of them could understand the words I used, but the whole group understood my actions. I worked to catch my breath. Decades of broadcast professionalism vanished in a single fit of rage.

And I felt the final symptom of my new disease: I felt exhilarated. People got that angry because getting that angry felt good.

Not just good, fantastic. Telling that horrid woman that she was a pawn that the agents of our country's demise used and then ridiculed felt fantastic.

In that five-minute interview, I learned why the homeless fight: because it feels better than getting victimized feels. Compared to being persecuted, fighting felt damn good.

LOS ANGELES, CALIFORNIA

Three days after Joanna Hayes won the Olympic Gold Medal for the 100-meter hurdles in Athens, Greece, I met her father, Ted Hayes, in a Los Angeles homeless shelter.

Ted founded the Dome Village, a shelter in Los Angeles built by and for the homeless. Ted became voluntarily homeless while Joanna was a young girl. He wanted to understand the "scourge" of homelessness so that he could better help to correct it.

Athletes who run track events work on speed and efficiency. They try to get around the track quicker than any of the other runners and without any stumbles or falls. A runner who runs the hurdle event has to also deal with impediments deliberately put in their way. They still try to get around the track the fastest, without tripping, but they knowingly undertake a task more difficult.

Joanna Hayes, the fastest and most successful runner in the world of the 2004 Olympics' 100-meter hurdles event, grew up with a dad who left mainstream life and calculatingly became homeless. A tall, fiercely intelligent and philosophical, strikingly handsome African-American man who might otherwise have passed through life with relatively few stumbles took the toughest course in life – on purpose.

My initial meeting with Ted Hayes happened about a month before the homeless tour began. We went by, in person, to ask permission to stay at his Dome Village. Our local Los Angeles contact, Ginny, had set up a meeting with Ted because when she called to ask permission for me to stay, the staff at the shelter said that they wanted to meet with me before they would decide.

Ted, very wary of having their work exploited for political gain, wanted to make sure that Ginny's description of me rang true. During our conversation that day he told me that he had lost faith in the political parties that had a reputation for sticking up for the poor. He said that the Democrats made promises that they don't keep and that he had become a Republican as a result of so many unfulfilled promises.

Ted told me that he became a Republican because it was, after all, the party that ended slavery. I looked around at the folks living with him in a parking lot filled with plastic domes and wanted to ask him if he really believed that slavery had ended.

What I said instead was, "You think the Democrats' concern for the poor is history and you embrace the fact that the Republicans ended slavery. But that was 150 years ago. That's history, too. Don't you think both of these parties have gotten pretty far away from their roots?"

He didn't answer. He took me into his dome dwelling, a circular house made of triangular panels fitted together at obtuse angles to each other to form an igloo-shaped structure. Inside his home/office hung dozens of pictures of him with different national and world leaders. On the door to the building he displayed a picture of himself with President George W. Bush.

I looked up at him and apologized in advance if I offended him in anyway, then asked, "I thought you didn't like being exploited for political gain?"

He replied that he would give the president the opportunity to prove what he was or wasn't capable of when it came to dealing with homeless issues. Ted said that he would drop the president too if he didn't prove himself to be a leader, truly concerned with ending the "scourge" of homelessness.

One of the ideas Ted promoted on his website was a cabinet-level position in the federal government dealing exclusively with homeless issues. No such position exists. I didn't ask him how long he was willing to wait for the president to prove what kind of leader he would be.

While Ted and I stood speaking, many Dome Village residents came by and introduced themselves to us. Children played around our feet. Small gardens and flowering areas, along with a few dozen trees, had been planted in the holes that the residents had made in the asphalt parking lot where their village stood.

Dome Village paid rent for the parking lot. Fundraising consumed a good deal of the time that Ted's staff spent working at the village.

The domes housed one or two groups of individuals. One dome had showers and toilets. Another dome contained the kitchen. The residents shared the chores.

All around the chainlink fence that bordered the parking lot homeless folks had set up camp. On the day that we arrived to meet Ted, the police interrogated the owners of one of these satellite dwellings. Ted told us that he wished that these other homeless folks would all just move along and squat somewhere else. Many of the perimeter residents turned tricks or sold drugs and he preferred that those things didn't happen around his shelter because they threatened the shelter's continued existence.

According to Ted, the biggest impediment to solving the problem of homelessness was that no one would acknowledge it as society's "scourge." People would speak in terms of charity assistance or laziness or mental illness, but Ted felt that these people missed the point.

Ted said that homeless people urinating on the sidewalk dehumanized the homeless after awhile and that society had to face that fact in a realistic and honest fashion. But not just because of the dehumanization: he felt that this behavior was bad for society as a whole.

Ted said that as long as homeless folks urinated in the entryway to the Hilton hotel, the whole dilemma of folks living in the street plagued the affluent as well. Ted felt it true enough that people shouldn't urinate in the streets because they are our neighbors and deserve to live better than that. But, he pointed out, it was just plain bad for business when businesses had to function in that sort of environment.

Justin, a little boy who lived with his mom in one of the domes, played at our feet as we spoke. He had a tricycle and got off of it periodically to push dirt around the openings in the asphalt through which a tree stood. His mom came by after a few minutes to collect him and we met her.

She held a baby girl, about six months old, in her arms and chatted with us in a warm and friendly manner. After Ted told her why we had come, that we wanted to return a month later and live in one of the domes, she invited us to live with her and her children.

She put the baby in my arms and brought us over to her dome so that we could see where they lived. Right behind her dome the village residents had a vegetable garden. She worked in it regularly. She loved fresh vegetables and she loved to garden.

Inside her dome they had a bunk bed and a small living area with a couch. A few triangular-shaped windows let the light into the room. And the space, while small, looked quite a bit like a home. It had blankets on the floor for the baby to play on and a television set to one side of the couch.

She said she'd love to have us stay with her, although she only had the bunk beds. I told her that I would bring a sleeping bag and spread out on the floor. While we talked, her baby had completely relaxed herself against me and had put her head down on my shoulder. I felt excited by the idea of returning to see this little family again.

PRESENTS

Ginny picked me up at the airport and drove downtown so that I could go shopping. I wanted to get some little presents for the children I would be staying with in the Dome Village shelter. As a rule, except for the collections we made for the shelters in general, I showed up each night empty-handed. But there was something special about staying with the little family I had met the month before my homeless journey began. I felt more like a visitor to old friends than a stranger dropping into an unknown scene.

Before we walked to the mall toy store, we stopped into a popular restaurant for lunch. Ginny, a young nicely dressed pretty woman accompanied by an apparent vagrant carrying a bedroll and her few belongings in a sack over one shoulder, requested a table for two.

They seated us at the far end of the restaurant. I felt like every occupant in the room stared at us as we walked by them. I knew I didn't fit the dress code that the other patrons had unofficially put into practice and speculated that this had caused the gawking. Additionally, during my recent travels, I had lost the ability to tell true perception from paranoia. I just couldn't tell for sure if my imagination created this perceived negative reaction on the part of the other restaurant diners or if they really had judged me as unfit to share their space.

I remembered some of the words of Ted Hayes from the month before when we last met. He said that to be around the homeless you had to have a special quality. People who spent time with the homeless had to be capable of loving the unlovable. Did I appear unlovable?

When the food came, I completely forgot about the other diners. Everything I ate tasted so indulgently delicious, I wouldn't have cared if they had thrown me out in the street as long as they let me take my plate with me.

After lunch we headed for the toy store, stopping briefly in a local department store to select the perfect outfit for a beautiful little girl. I agonized over the correct size, wanting her to wear it right away. When I got to the toys, I headed straight for the trucks. From the moment I had seen Justin pushing dirt around the trees with his hands, I knew he needed a bulldozer or a back-hoe.

Later, when we arrived at the dome where I would spend the night, I realized what a fool I was. My judgmental brain had failed me and I had blundered dismally by making these purchases. I had visited the Dome Village early in the day the last time. The return trip placed me at their home at about 8 p.m.

I walked into the dome, my purchases in my arms and didn't find what I expected to find. The woman I thought would be sitting there with her two children was actually surrounded by children. She didn't have two kids, she had eight!

I felt awful. I gave the babies their gifts and walked over to meet the rest of her children with nothing to give them. How could I have been so certain that she only had two children? How could I have made such a mistake? How did they all live in this tiny area? And how could they all sleep on the bunk beds?

For starters, they didn't all sleep on the bunk bed. Mom and the baby slept on the couch together and the rest of the children who slept in the dome, slept in the bunk beds together. Two of her older boys no longer lived with their mom. They had just come by to meet me. A third older boy had a little time left in prison.

The middle children, the ones between the ages of the babies I had already met and the older kids who had relocated to other housing or prison, all attended school locally. Two of the boys looked like twins. The older of the look-alike kids had just turned 12 and had scads of homework to get done before he could go to sleep that night.

His mom kept interrupting him to do chores. She had him run to get water and other things that they needed for the evening in the dome. His oldest brother who had come by to visit yelled at her to stop giving the younger boy so many chores. The oldest looked at me and said, "He'll never get good grades if she doesn't stop bothering him. Then he'll end up like me. I got no job and I can't get one. I'll never be anything. My brother is smart and he likes to study, he could get out of here."

I asked the studious boy what he wanted to do. He said, "I just want to live where there aren't any basket-pushers." He meant grocery carts with homeless people pushing them around town. He wanted to go to the University of Southern California and get a degree and move as far away from basket-pushers as he could get.

I had just hopscotched my way across the country staying with homeless folks. He would have to learn how to eliminate homelessness in the United States if he really wanted to stay in this country and get far away from the homeless.

I offered to help him with his homework but he declined. He said that he could get it done on his own.

The mom of all these kids spent her day looking for an apartment. She had $600 a month available to pay rent. She found a place that she really liked. It had a stove. Most of the apartments in her price range had only hot plates for cooking. The landlord hadn't impressed her and the neighborhood lacked security, but there would be more room than they were used to in the dome – and the kids could have some privacy.

Still, she didn't think that she would get the place. The line of folks who had wanted to see it snaked out the door of the building. She lamented how difficult it was to find housing. She knew that Ted wanted to free up her dome to help somebody new. Ted had an unwritten policy not to keep folks "forever." He wanted to help folks get back on their feet, but once there, they were expected to use those feet to get out of the shelter.

I held the baby all night. At first I just held her for fun. But the mom looked so relieved to have her hands free and to be relaxing on the couch by herself that I just kept the baby with me all night. She slept on my chest.

Early the next morning I gave the baby back to her mom. I told her that I had a plane to catch and my hostess got very upset. She wanted me to see what her day was like and I was going to miss the whole thing.

I apologized. I explained that my system of stepping into people's lives clearly missed the vast majority of the story, but I had commitments in the next town on the tour. She accused me of leaving her the same way that a man leaves her: abruptly the next morning.

She elaborated, "I have no use for men. Except for sex. That's where I got my babies. Sex and babies, that's all anyone needs a man for."

I walked out to Ginny's car feeling like a failure. I had completely stiffed at least three school-aged kids on presents. I left the mom who had so generously invited us into her existence feeling like I didn't care about her life. I looked back and saw one of the oldest boys waving and proudly wearing my pullover fleece jacket. I had taken it off when I climbed into my sleeping bag. I waved and smiled back. "There," I thought, "at least one more of them got a present."

When Ginny and I got to her car, we found that she had left it unlocked. The car, unmolested, remained parked where we had left it. Just two blocks from skid row, nobody messed with Ginny's new car. Ted Hayes commanded respect. No matter how tough the neighborhood, respect is respect.

Ginny drove me back to LAX. Ted Hayes had voluntarily lived homeless for more than 20 years. I had four more nights to go. The 100-meter hurdles event of my lifetime, and I felt sore from tripping over the Los Angeles hurdle.

A PLACE OF THEIR OWN

At the turn of the twenty-first century, the homeless in Portland, Oregon, marched in a parade. It was a parade of their own making. The homeless pushed shopping carts instead of riding on floats and they used the event to call attention to the fact that they had nowhere to go.

In most communities being homeless is synonymous with being unwanted. The authorities, working on behalf of the communities, try to move the homeless population off the street. If shelters harbor disease or danger, or simply don't exist, the homeless become nomads. A person without shelter wanders the streets and parking lots, settling occasionally, then relocating again as soon as the authorities find them and evict them.

The homeless of Portland, Oregon, organized themselves into a cohesive and communicative body. Together they demanded a piece of land upon which they might build a community. The shopping cart parade underscored their solidarity and ability to work together. Consequently, the residents of Portland agreed with the homeless demonstrators that they should have a place of their own.

On December 16, 2000, a piece of municipal land, several acres in size, was allotted to the homeless protesters and a tent village immediately sprung into place. The organizers of the settlement drafted guidelines by which the community would govern itself. And all residents signed a contract before they could live there. The new village's inhabitants would have to be over eighteen years of age and agree not to hurt themselves or each other.

Most of the homeless that participated in the program had jobs and some of them had cars. A cooperative was established and while none of the inhabitants had the financial resources to access traditional housing in the area, many of them were extremely industrious and began building more permanent structures. Within a few months the tents gave way to shanties and Dignity Village became a fixture.

By the fall of 2004, the village had completely surrounded itself with a barricade of sorts. The main entrance had a guard shack at the opening and the residents staffed the compound 24 hours a day.

Those living outside its perimeter did not always share the sense of dignity the residents felt inside the village. 'Hoodlums' and 'punks' had attacked the community on several occasions and a couple of times they had fire bombed the place.

"The sturdy beggars protect the deserving poor," that's what Jack Tafari told me when I walked in through the entry way to the village. Although this population clearly governed itself by general consensus, they also had a leader.

Jack described the constant threat of violence that hung over their heads as residents of Portland's newest type of community. He was quick to point out, however, that in most homeless communities the threat of violence comes from both inside and outside the group. At Dignity Village, violence perpetrated from within the organization had been virtually eliminated.

Jack explained, "Most women are raped within 11 days of becoming homeless, no one here has ever been raped." He went on to describe their place as a "Rastafarian-based Jeffersonian community. Everyone here is treated with dignity. Dignis means 'human worth,' and everyone here must acknowledge their own human worth as well as the value of others."

A woman who stood with us as we spoke added, "Some people come here not knowing what any of this means. The first

thing people who come here have to do is unlearn lying. They
had to deceive the whole time they were on the street; here they
don't have to lie anymore."

"We give them three months to transition. If they can't do it
in that time, they have to go," Jack further explained. Then he
looked across the village and added, "That's an awful lot to learn
in just three months, how to be part of a functioning cooperative
community. It would be like giving someone just three months
to become a doctor."

Waste wood gets dumped at Dignity Village all the time.
Even things as big as old boat docks find their way to the capable
hands of the craftsmen and women in the group. They pull the
nails and remove the other metal fixtures; then all the wood gets
reused to build structures on the premises.

Approximately sixty people lived there in 2004. Most of
them lived in little shanty huts. A few cob houses built of straw
bales stood in various stages of construction. All of the dwellings were undergoing a jacking process to lift them two feet or
so above the asphalt.

"We have to get these houses off the pallets upon which they
were originally built. The houses sit too close to the ground.
The cats can't get under them to do their work." Jack spoke as
he pointed to a rat the size of a cat waddling along the side of a
woodpile. "The rats can squeeze under the houses but the cats
can't get in after them."

Approximately every three shanties along the pathway inside
the village, the residents had built a fire station. They used
bathtubs or fifty-five gallon drums to collect rain in case of fire.
Because of the rainy climate of Portland, Oregon, they never ran
out of water. Each fire station also had a regulation multi type fire
extinguisher, incase the fire involved chemicals or electrical devises.

Each station had a first aid kit, incase of injury. Since the fire
bombings, the sturdy beggars decided that the deserving poor
might sustain injuries too immediate for the local authorities'
normal response time. The first aid kits assured some assistance
to the afflicted while they waited for the first responders to arrive.

Dignity Village had limited electrical power. Small windmills supplied some electricity and they powered the pathway lighting and the library.

Even though the village had chemical toilets located at one end of the development, the entire compound had that fetid smell of human waste. That smell coupled with the odor and commotion caused by the many cats chasing rats in the vicinity created the only truly unpleasant aspect of the settlement.

Supposedly William Shakespeare was arrested and briefly incarcerated for building his dung heap too close to his house. Is this just medieval urban legend? Or could it be that the close proximity to such putrid smells makes poets of men?*

*Dignity Village publishes its poetry on the World Wide Web.

WATCH OUT FOR THE RATS

Maybe it was sleep deprivation. Maybe my experiences had blurred the line between normalcy and irony. Maybe what seemed right to me had become wrong. Or maybe I no longer knew the difference. Maybe it was just that I had survived eleven days homeless. Maybe surpassing the magic number that Jack Tafari, the director of Dignity Village, said was the usual number of days it took a homeless woman to get raped –without getting raped- had made me giddy. I don't know what caused it, but walking up to Dignity Village and seeing its placement in the cosmos made me feel like somebody, probably me, had lost track of reality.

Dignity Village stood on land gifted to the homeless by the city of Portland. There's an old saying where I come from, "You know what you get for nothin' don't ya? Nothin'!"

I walked to the guardhouse at the entryway and signed in as a guest. To my left side as I faced the village stretched a long tall chain linked fence. At the top of the fence, at least 12 feet high, coiled a length of razor wire that spanned the entire fence structure.

The city had put the huge fence in, not to keep the villagers inside their compound, nor to keep them safe from the vandals that tried to burn their village down, but to keep the occupants on the other side of the fencing from going anywhere.

Dignity Village had been built on the property adjacent to the minimum-security prison in Portland, Oregon.

I stood there staring at the fence, at the elevated guard posts, at the bright courtyard lights, and at the secure doors and windows. My mind couldn't imagine any fiction as wacky as this improbable truth. This structure – that controlled all personal behavior and eliminated nearly all interaction with the opposite sex yet provided three square meals and protection from the elements – sat along side Dignity Village.

And Dignity Village, where people came to live as unencumbered as any ordinary person might in the United States of America, had no protection from the elements. The residents were vulnerable to the actions of passers by or each other. Control and governance were made by consensus and obeyed by universal accord. Noncompliance with rules resulted in expulsion not continued incarceration.

Freedom must have taunted the inmates who looked out of their windows at the village's openness. Hunger, rat bites, and cold served as the price of the villagers' self-determination. Still any of the homeless at Dignity Village could have, with one simple illegal act, exchanged their independence for the warmth and stability of the neighboring community.

Our criminals live better than the poor.

"Watch out for the rats, they're as big as cats and there are more of them," cautioned my host.

"Where do they come from?" I asked. Now a veteran of so many different types of shelters and having never seen even a third as many rats, I didn't know why such a large number existed here and not in other places.

"Oh, they're our other neighbors. When the government gave us the land, they set us next to the compost pile for the city. Rats and compost just go hand and hand."

Back home we have an old saying, "You know what you get for nothin' don't ya?"

LIBRARY

I took my bag of things after I got my sleeping bag and pillow out of it and I propped it against the library door.

Originally the library traveled the city streets picking up passengers and delivering them to other points on the public transportation route. Now, all four tires nearly flat, the bus had books and a television with a videocassette player and a collection of videotapes too.

Some of the narrow benches lined the walls of the bus; others stuck out into the aisle. I didn't mind sleeping anywhere anymore, but I wasn't too excited about having any of the local rat population share my space. I took a few of the books and wedged them between my bag and the stairs in the entryway of the bus just in case the rats were strong enough to push the door open with just the weight of my dirty clothes in the way.

I had flown through Hurricane Jean. I landed in Los Angeles as an earthquake shook the runway. And earlier that day as I landed in Portland Oregon, I watched Mount St. Helens erupt for the first time in nearly 20 years. I had lived through the trifecta of natural disasters on this trip across country and I had no intention of being gnawed to death by tiny rodent teeth in a dilapidated school bus.

I chuckled myself to sleep as I visualized my body found by the authorities. I could see it in my mind's eye: hundreds of little bite marks, my form all contorted and surrounded by some of my best friends. Friends, with whom I would ordinarily be spending the night in my quiet room in Maine: Chaucer, Steinbeck, Arthur Miller... only my favorite local author and good friend, Stephen King, would have been impressed by the way in which I departed. Oh, maybe him and Edgar Allen Poe.

I chuckled again and hoped that these musings didn't turn into dreams. I really had all the frightening stuff I could handle during my days.

CHICAGO, ILLINOIS

We don't make $5.50 an hour. That's what Mexicans make.
We can't afford to make wages like those. The Mexicans work at
a McDonald's around here, and even though they might be home-
less too, at least they, when they send half their money home, it
makes their families at home rich. We could work for those awful
wages too, but nobody we know would live better for it.

McDonald's jobs, those are for Mexicans.

Those are the words three very pretty women sitting with
their children in the back kitchen of a women's shelter used
when they shared their take on minimum wage jobs in Illinois.

If you believe the late singer/song writer, Jim Croce, I was
in, "the baddest part of town." This women-and-children-only
shelter was located on the south side of Chicago in a building
that looked small from the street, but once inside had a great
deal of room.

After entering through the front foyer we walked into a chapel. Our Chicago supporters had spent weeks collecting makeup
and toiletries, sanitary products and hair accessories. About 10
of them accompanied me to the shelter to drop these items off,
hoping to meet some of the occupants and voice their desire to
continue working for and with the shelter.

The director, a female minister who had devoted her life to
helping other women in need, sat with us in the chapel and received the gifts. She told the local people that accompanied me

that they would not be allowed into the shelter with me: that this common area was as far as they could go.

I think some of my companions were disappointed, but they all respected her desire to protect the privacy of the residents.

She asked if we would pray with her. We all bowed our heads and she prayed, thanking God for the items we brought to the shelter and imploring Him to end this sort of poverty in our country.

My supporters took me aside as they left the shelter. Charles, the chief organizer of the event, looked at me sternly and told me that he would be back in the morning about 6 a.m. He spoke harshly to me and warned me not to go outside the building no matter what my reasons. He said that he would come inside the doorway to get me. Under no circumstances was I to wait outside the building!

He cautioned, "I don't care if this place burns down, I want you to stay inside."

We both chuckled but he'd made his point. Charles didn't think the neighborhood was a good place for a middle-aged white woman to be and he didn't want me testing his theory.

After they left, the minister took me back behind the Chapel and her whole demeanor changed.

Realistically, the same negative attitude I was about to receive from the people in this Chicago shelter could have lurked under the more friendly demeanors that other area shelter staff and residents had exhibited toward me. However, if the other folks I had encountered over the past week and a half likewise disapproved of my visit, they didn't let it show. But at this particular shelter, condemnation, cynicism and contempt poured out of most of these folks from the moment my supporters left the place.

There were two exceptions to the hostility that I experienced at the shelter. One woman, an employee had stayed late to show me around. She told me how excited she got when she learned that I wanted to come and learn about their facility. Clearly proud of the work they got done with the little that they had, she took me through the back rooms explaining their operation.

She ran the kitchen. Sparkling clean and stocked with canned goods, they prepared three meals a day on weekdays for the residents. The night I stayed there was a Sunday night, so the patrons had gotten their own meals. When we walked into the walk-in fridge, she said that the women sometimes pick through the food left back there, but that they really were encouraged to spend their weekends visiting their families and friends.

Each resident could stay up to four months. They could use the time to find jobs or make some other sort of plans. The minister told us during our orientation that 70 percent of the women that came to her shelter had no education. They hadn't even finished high school. She added that most of the women she cared for couldn't get jobs without educations and basically wound up on public assistance or worse.

After my tour of the kitchen I went back out to the common area. The second friendly woman came to my rescue when the other women told me that they didn't know why I decided to visit them, but they didn't think it was anything but garbage. They told me that I wouldn't learn anything from visiting shelters. They said that I could bring a few tampons and some mascara and feel better about myself, but it wouldn't enhance my appreciation of their lives.

The minister sat there with the other women who had explained to me the Mexican employment situation. They asked me a few questions about the other parts of my trip. I told them about Los Angeles and how naïve I had been about the mom with eight kids and I agreed with them about my lack of understanding. I told them how happy I had been to see one of the older kids wearing my jacket and that I had felt terrible about singling some of the children out for gifts and neglecting the others.

They all started to laugh. They were laughing at me. I sat there mystified by their guffaws. Finally one of the women solved the riddle for me. "You didn't give him your jacket because you wanted him to have something. You gave it to him because you were scared to take it back."

She shocked me. I couldn't believe my ears. I must have looked like a dog with his head cocked off sideways in disbelief. I told her that I didn't think so: that I didn't remember feeling afraid. I searched my mind to remember the feeling I had when I saw the young man in my jacket. I told her that I distinctly remember feeling relieved and happy.

The minister spoke then. She told me that I was afraid of black people and that I didn't even know it. She said that my fear ran so deep that I could convince myself that it didn't exist. I wanted to tell her about growing up in a project and living with black folks; that I could never remember feeling frightened. But I knew it would sound lame, like my trip across the country sounded lame to these women.

And I couldn't be sure she wasn't right. I didn't think I was afraid of any kind of people. I thought that all races and colors and religions and every other sort of group had some great people and some frightening people, but what did I know?

I sat there, certain that Attila the Hun, Goering, the creep who shot Medgar Evers and all those racist folks thought that they were on the right track too. And hadn't Charles vehemently lectured me about going outside? How could I defend myself?

I sat there, wearing the cheap jacket I had purchased to replace the one I had lost in Los Angeles, exhausted, beating myself up for even attempting this ridiculous homeless tour. They were right, except for a few tampons and a couple of bed sheets and some food in some pantries, what had I done?

I missed my kids. I felt horrible.

Humans are after all, just animals. If you go to a chicken coop to see a wounded chicken, you better look quickly. The other animals will take that injured bird and peck it to pieces. In a matter of minutes that weak member of the flock will vanish, nothing but a few left over feathers and some bloody beaks.

A tall slender very quiet proud hen at the end of the room, sitting with her young chicks on her lap, came to my rescue.

"Hey," she said, "come on, I'll show you where we sleep, you can pick out a bunk."

THE ONLY PILLOW

The furthest room back from the street, and about the same size as the chapel, housed approximately 18 wooden bunk beds. Made from rough 2x4 pieces of wood, each bunk had a twin bed mattress.

Under and around the beds, the women and children stowed their personal belongings. The room had the appearance of a chaotic military barracks. The bunk beds lined the length of the walls on either side of the room, with personal items haphazardly strewn all around them.

Inside the dormitory, several women sat on their beds. It had gotten late and in spite of the bright lighting, most of the children had fallen asleep. Many of the moms out back spoke quietly among themselves. None of these women knew who I was, or why I was there.

My guardian who saved me from my emotional self-immolation said that it had been years since she, and probably any of the other women there, had seen a white woman in their neighborhood that wasn't on a billboard advertisement. She said that I probably made the women in the kitchen a little defensive.

I selected a bed between two already occupied bunks. On one side a woman with two young children lay awake with her eyes closed. She spoke to me but didn't open her eyes until I spoke back.

This was her first night in that particular shelter. She and her kids had been three days on the street before someone told her about this mission and the minister who made it possible. She told me that she hadn't slept while she and her kids had been on the street and was finding it hard to get to sleep now that she could. She explained her deprivation; "You can't sleep homeless with babies. Not if you don't want anyone to hurt them."

On the other side of me a woman shared her bed with just one child. Her child had that signature terrible cough.

I started to unpack my sleeping bag when the woman who had brought me out back asked me if I liked to read.

I stated that I did and she showed me the book that she and her children were reading. They read together every night. I volunteered to read for a while, but she said that the children had to do the reading that night. Her grammar-school-aged kids read to us for about a half hour.

Finally their mom turned to me and told me that she had a college degree. That she could do secretarial work and that she had applied for a job with Catholic Charities. She said that her interview went well and that she really hoped they might hire her. She told me that she had often gotten pretty good jobs, but that her family was 'dysfunctional.' Her parents, she explained, would never let her just work. They called her all the time and hassled her. She explained that she couldn't remember a time growing up that her parents didn't work their hardest to ruin her life.

She said that sometimes she wished she could leave town and not tell them where she went, but they were her parents and she couldn't turn her back on them.

She looked up at me, the book her children had been reading across her lap, and asked, "Can't an employer just understand when a person's family is crazy and overlook it? Can't one employer understand how hard it is to work to bring up your kids differently from how you were brought up, but not turn your back on the ones before you who tried their best?"

If this had been the first night of my trip I might have asked her where this family was now. Why was she in a homeless shelter unless it was because they had turned their backs on her? These questions came into my head but they didn't seem helpful. I listened to her a while longer and when she finished venting; I went to my bed to lie down.

I woke up in the middle of the night because the child next to me couldn't stop coughing. I looked over as another woman rummaged through her bag and brought out a bottle of cough medicine.

Someone had turned out the lights, but some sort of night light glowed and I could see the others in their beds.

I realized that I had the only pillow in the room. I leaned over to the mom of the sick child and gave her my pillow. I told her that I usually propped my kids' heads up when they coughed and it had always seemed to help.

Later that morning when I went out front to wait for my ride, I saw the little girl sleeping on her new pillow. The cough medicine had worked. I felt better about it all. And I felt pretty sure that I hadn't given up my jacket out of fear. But I just couldn't tell for sure.

FLOWERS

    I stood inside the doorway as instructed by Charles. In the foyer I sat in a chair at a small table. The night watchman for the shelter sat with me. He was about 60 years old and had a sweet friendly face. He asked me questions about my trip. The watchman's calm demeanor and gentle way relaxed me as we spoke.

    He told me that he really loved the woman who ran the shelter. He thought that the minister cared a great deal about the community. He didn't know if she did the wonderful things she did for God or for the women – he just knew that she got an awful lot of good stuff done.

    He asked me if I had a husband. "Not any more," I answered.

    He believed that was wrong and he told me why.

    That's the problem today. People aren't married anymore. Married people have each other and you are never alone when trouble hits. These women in here need husbands, somebody to take care of them.

    I figured a bunch of those women did have husbands, or had one at one time, but not the kind the night watchman described. Sometimes, I thought, the trouble that hits comes from the person who promised to love you forever.

    He then explained God to me. He said he knew people thought God would correct the problems that existed in places like this shelter on the south side of Chicago. But that his little shelter must look pretty insignificant from where God sits.

Think of all the shelters on the planet. And just think, there could be an awful lot of planets like this one in our universe. And it's the religious people that tell us God's interfering in our lives and going to set things right. But God's probably made many more universes than just ours. So all these shelters on earth, all these earths, and a whole pile more universes, it doesn't look like God will answer the religious peoples' prayers any time soon.

Then he told me that he hadn't had much opportunity to talk with a white woman and he had some things to share.

We need to look out for each other. We need to be open to the help that comes to us no matter what shape or form it takes. And we need to pay attention to the color of the flowers. If religious people know God made the flowers, then they have to know that He made them different colors for a good reason. Just like he made us different colors. And I think a flower's pretty no matter what color it is, don't you?

I agreed. I told him I liked flowers of all different colors and people of all different colors.

Charles walked through the door to get me and the night watchman told me goodbye. As I walked outside he called after me, "Now when you are done with this trip I want you to go home and get married. You need somebody to look after you."

I smiled at him and I smiled at his wisdom. While I doubted I'd run home and get a husband, I couldn't agree more with his observation about people needing each other.

And I liked the way he described our differences. People are like flowers: different colors for a reason.

DETROIT, MICHIGAN

"Every top has to sit on it's own bottom." That's the motto that Gina Harris, my host at COTS, used to describe the philosophy of their not-for-profit organization that serves the homeless in Detroit, Michigan.

COTS, while not a government agency, incorporates government programs and uses government funding in conjunction with private sector donations.

Detroit has many kinds of shelters. Short term accommodations, warming centers, soup kitchens, multi-purpose and long term housing all combine to make Detroit the most no-nonsense city on my trip when it comes to working with a population that has no where to live. The goal in Detroit is not housing people. The goal in Detroit is eliminating homelessness.

I stayed in a multi-purpose shelter. If you have ever watched an episode of the old M*A*S*H program that aired on television you know what it was like to be in this shelter with me.

Folks that showed up for help went through a diagnosis process. First a pre-screening took place, much like the triage of the M*A*S*H television show. In the program, the wounded would be brought to the military hospital and the most distressed would get immediate attention.

Everyone shows up on a shelter doorstep for a reason. In Detroit, they found out what that reason was before they sent a person through a certain regimen inside the system.

The shelter where I stayed had been one of Detroit's old hotels. Many of the fixtures remained from when the occupants of the building were paying guests stopping into Detroit for a visit. The elevators still had much of their old filigree ornamenting them. Above the elevator doors, a numbered half circle with an arrow rolling right to left and back again told you which floor the elevator was at along its trip inside the building.

At quick glance I half expected Frank Sinatra or Jimmy Stewart to exit the elevator when the doors opened. The lobby of this shelter had the air of a black and white movie set mingled with a Social Security waiting room.

The old hotel restaurant served as a dining facility for the residents. The meals were cooked in the same kitchen that for decades had satisfied patrons of the hotel. Before and after meals the dining area became a meeting place. AA meetings and NA meetings happened nearly every day.

The many floors of the structure allowed for a certain amount of segregation of the residents as needed. Some floors housed men only. They had floors for families with children. While several states kept homeless moms and kids together, I hadn't stayed in a shelter until this one, that allowed homeless single dads to keep their kids with them. Dads got to continue parenting in Detroit.

Because the rooms used to be hotel rooms, they each had a bathroom. People had privacy. Even those rooms that housed several single persons granted more individual privacy than most shelters, because instead of a whole floor sharing a bathroom, only the occupants of one room did.

Folks who made it to this shelter could settle down for a while. They could unpack their belongings and put the soap and shampoo away.

Each floor had a common area. Guests could watch television or play board games. On the family floor, small children and babies could come together to play.

The facility had a clinic. Prescription drugs were kept safe and first aid was administered to those who got injured or felt mildly ill. Unlike other shelters, this facility stayed open 24 hours a day. They had an in-house employment center complete with resume-writing assistance, job placement, and computer training. It had homework clubs that school-aged kids were expected to attend.

Gina, the director, explained that poverty drove many people to homelessness, but numerous others became down and out by making the wrong choices. Once the staff assessed a person's needs, the shelter supported them by meeting those needs and providing some stability. Then the residents could learn to make better choices.

Gina said, "The shock of whatever they went through on the street ends when they get here. Once their necessities are met, they become free to concentrate on other things. To prepare for a better life."

Profile statistics had changed a great deal in the homeless population since COTS began. At first their clientele was older and more of them were men. Jill, the woman responsible for managing and raising the funds necessary to keep COTS open, explained that the foster system had become a contributing factor to the changing demographic of the homeless population. Once kids turned 18, they were released from the foster care system, resulting in more homelessness.

She said that these kids are sent into the world with very few of the skills they need to survive in it. And for the most part they have no family to fall back on in hard times. The government had become their family. Then the government tossed them out on their own after high school, with nowhere to return to if the kids found that they couldn't make it alone.

The safety net most families provide to kids just starting out doesn't exist for children from foster care. There's no place for them to go if they falter along their way to self-sufficiency.

COTS sheltered, in the traditional sense, only those who specifically could not or would not be helped any other way. And a different facility located up the street took care of those folks.

All other homeless individuals and families that came to COTS were set on a course to independence. In the mean time, the COTS program worked diligently to provide interim and transitional housing.

People also learned skills they might not already have: Balancing a checkbook, budgeting for bills, accessing daycare, these vital components to everyday living were taught to people staying inside the COTS facilities.

Any resident who had an income, whether a paycheck or an assistance check, was expected to open a bank account. The staff at COTS monitored the balance and helped them learn to manage and plan using money they themselves had saved. A key first step to having a place of one's own was having a savings account to finance it.

This close monitoring of finances didn't end when a resident finally moved out on their own. The staff at COTS welcomed questions and helped solve problems from former residents for up to a year after they left the facility.

"It's a lot easier for us to keep them on their feet when their only problem is a fuel bill that they can't afford," Jill explained. "If they wait until all their bills are late and they are getting evicted, we end up back where we started. We'd rather help keep them on their feet than have to keep resetting them on their feet."

New educational tools, learning new life style habits, kicking an addiction, all necessities of "sitting your top on your own bottom," all available at COTS.

Why did Detroit have such a system, and so many other places have nothing even like it?

"Political will," Gina told me. "We had a mayor who wanted to end homelessness and wouldn't take 'No' for an answer."

COLEMAN YOUNG

Coleman Young, the Detroit mayor elected to his first of four terms in 1973 didn't want folks freezing in the streets. Young, one of the famous Tuskegee Airmen, a labor organizer and an ardent civil rights leader made eradicating homelessness a prime concern of his administration. The other members of his city council did not share his priorities. Young had to win over these other lawmakers before he could accomplish his mission.

As Gina told me the story, she explained that leadership isn't getting folks to do what they already want to do. It's getting them to do what they don't want to do.

Downtown Detroit had a public building named for the Ford Motor Company. It had been closed for a number of years when Young became mayor. On one particularly frigid night he had it reopened as a warming center for those on Detroit's streets who struggled against the cold.

Having so many poor people in one place highlighted the problem and brought the topic to the forefront of the voters' minds. Gina believed that this single act, opening this warming shelter, turned the hearts and minds of enough other council members for Young to gain the support he needed.

Gina couldn't say whether the other city officials backed his ideas because of some newly acquired understanding and compassion or because they feared political backlash. She didn't care either way. To her, it was enough to know that a number of Detroit's other leaders supported Young's initiatives and they began addressing homelessness aggressively.

Gina told me the Coleman Young story as she drove me to a transitional housing center. We walked up to the front steps and waited for security to open the door.

The large brick building, impeccably kept, housed women and their children who graduated from the triage shelter and needed apartments. The doorways, windows, and trim-work on the structure looked like white marble and featured designs and filigree. The building had been a gift from the Roman Catholic Church.

The Catholic Church had donated a great deal of property to the COTS program, the former convent we toured as well as other residences. And the large motor companies of the motor city had funded many of the renovations and related programs. What Coleman Young started eventually evolved into a multifaceted organization supported by many community leaders.

Gina believed that the government had enormous capacity to correct society's ills. She said that when people who have homes gain an understanding of what life is like for those who don't have homes, the government has won the battle. She said, "People urinate in the streets because they live in the streets." She elaborated that once lawmakers and voters understand that reality, people urinating in the streets isn't disgusting. A society where people live in the streets is what's disgusting.

Gina took me by one more shelter in the consortium. It housed the transients who refused to be identified or take part in the long-range rehabilitation offered at the other shelters. These residents could only stay one night at a time and the facility lacked the accoutrements or security of the other places we had visited.

Gina said that originally she had planned to bring me there as well, but decided against it. She felt that I would be both repulsed and defenseless staying in that particular facility. I thought of mentioning the shelter in New York City where I had felt both those things and more. I hesitated because I hated those feelings so much. If I told her that I could handle being in a shelter that bad, then my fear was that she might take me up on it and make me spend another night in a shelter that ghastly. One of those experiences felt like plenty in a lifetime.

As I reconsidered my reluctance, Gina continued to speak. "It's locked down anyway. The homeless still go in there, but they are discouraging anyone else from coming there for a while. One of the attendants got stabbed to death two nights ago. The woman had psychotic episodes. She doesn't remember killing him. She didn't even know him. His funeral is tomorrow."

COUCH SURFING IN OHIO

Before daylight the next day, my ride came to get me. I had slept on an orange vinyl couch in the seventh floor playroom. Like so many other cities, the shelters of Detroit had no empty beds. I stopped by the clinic to pick up my prescription medicines. For safety sake, all shelter residents surrendered them upon arrival.

I went by car to Cleveland. Glad to be through flying for a couple of days, different volunteer drivers handed me off from one to the other like a baton in a relay race.

We arrived in Ohio on the last voter registration day for the 2004 presidential election. Ohio had a 30-day waiting period for voter registration. Campaign workers from the various progressive groups throughout the state had worked feverishly for months to increase voter registration among the poor.

Several states appeared capable of tipping the scales in one direction or another on Election Day. Florida, New Mexico and Ohio among the most undecided of the states that had large numbers of electoral votes.

Congressman Dennis Kucinich's office had connected us with different homeless advocates and we had arranged to meet with them upon our arrival in the city. Because it was such a critical date, electorally speaking, we had to drop in on one of their "get out the vote" organizational meetings. Now that so many new registrants existed, the big challenge remained getting them to the polls to vote.

It had been prearranged that I would sleep at a woman's domestic violence shelter. Our supporters in the area had collected many items for them, but because of intense security measures employed by this shelter, we were not allowed to bring them there. We took them instead to the local Salvation Army.

On our way back from the donation drop-off, we got a call from the advocate Kucinich had directed us to, informing us that the domestic violence shelter had reached capacity for the night. He offered to keep trying to place me and stated that they might be able to rearrange things to make room for me.

Our No. 1 rule was in danger of being violated. We had promised from the start not to put anyone out of a bed.

My campaign connection in Ohio made a suggestion, "Why don't you sleep on my couch. Couch surfing is done all the time by the homeless." He was right, but it felt like a copout. I mentioned that I could stay in a park. He continued, "You don't need to stay in a park, you can sleep on the couch. If you want authenticity, I can tell you about when I was homeless."

His parents had split up when he was a kid. He didn't want to go with one of them and he couldn't go with the other. So he just struck out on his own. I took a step back staring at this young man dressed professionally with his dark blue suit, short haircut and clean-shaven face and tried to picture him as a homeless teen.

I slept on his couch that night and he told me about his struggle. His stories were sad. But he had gotten back on his feet. And now he was taking care of me.

Oct. 5 is the day I ended my homeless experience. Tracey, the woman who had come to my rescue when I lost my passport, had flown into Cleveland to bring me notes from my kids, clean clothes and my makeup.

Marnie and Dean, two campaign staffers for the Vice Presidential race, had also flown into town. But they came to help me prepare for the debates that were scheduled for later that evening. After renting a hotel room, we all went out to lunch and they prepped me on world and national news events I had

missed over the last few weeks and quizzed me on issues I needed to know. Like tutors for a big test, they shifted my thoughts
from the very visceral to intellectual.

Dick Cheney and John Edwards had been invited by Case
Western University to debate each other in an event that would
be broadcast live around the country.

Four other candidates for Vice President had their names
on the ballot in enough states to secure the requisite number of
electoral votes to win the election if they carried those states. I
was one of those candidates. But because we had little funding
and were not part of the mainstream political scene, we were not
invited to participate in the Case Western debate.

So across town from Case Western, in a West Side suburb of
Cleveland, at Baldwin-Wallace College a debate was held for us.
The Reform Party candidate couldn't make it. But the Libertar-
ian and Constitution candidates were there.

The format was simple. We debated many important issues
facing the United States for an hour and a half. Then we joined
the audience that had come to see us. Together we watched the
debate as it was broadcast from Case Western on large-screen
television sets that had been set up for the event.

Hundreds of people filled the Baldwin-Wallace auditorium.
I sat there, alongside the other two VP candidates and watched
Gwen Ifill from National Public Broadcasting ask Cheney and
Edwards questions about their foreign and domestic policies.

At the very end of the program, Gwen shifted gears in the
questioning and brought up the topic of AIDS. She directed the
question to Mr. Cheney, the man who's getting the new underground
bunker built at the Vice Presidential mansion in Washington,
D.C., and she told him of the shocking statistics around young
African American women and AIDS.

IFILL: "I will talk to you about health care, Mr. Vice President. You have two minutes. But in particular, I want to talk to
you about AIDS, and not about AIDS in China or Africa, but
AIDS right here in this country, where black women between

the ages of 25 and 44 are 13 times more likely to die of the disease than their counterparts."

"What should the government's role be in helping to end the growth of this epidemic?"

"Thirteen times more likely to die," she said. And she wanted an answer about this horrific statistic from the man just one heartbeat away from becoming the most powerful man in the world.

I thought about Boston. I thought about the man I met who worked with young women to educate them about this epidemic. I was betting that he knew more about the plague upon African-American women then their Vice President did.

And Mr. Cheney responded to Gwen Ifill; first disregarding her request that he not discuss the situations in foreign countries.

CHENEY: "Well, this is a great tragedy, Gwen, when you think about the enormous cost here in the United States and around the world of the AIDS epidemic – pandemic, really. Millions of lives lost, millions more infected and facing a very bleak future."

"In some parts of the world, we've got the entire, sort of, productive generation has been eliminated as a result of AIDS, all except for old folks and kids – nobody to do the basic work that runs an economy."

"The president has been deeply concerned about it. He has moved and proposed and gotten through the Congress authorization for $15 billion to help in the international effort, to be targeted in those places where we need to do everything we can, through a combination of education as well as providing the kinds of medicines that will help people control the infection."

And finally he addressed her point,

"Here in the United States, we've made significant progress. I have not heard those numbers with respect to African-American women. I was not aware that it was – that they're in epidemic there..."

No, Mr. Vice President not "there." HERE.

ACKNOWLEDGEMENTS

So many wonderful people made this trip possible. I want to thank all the shelters, their directors, and their staff people.

Thanks to all the volunteers on the ground who met my flights or trains or drove me from place to place. They fed me and helped me stay on schedule and kept me safe.

My running mate, Presidential Candidate David Cobb, who wholeheartedly supported focusing my half of the campaign on issues involving the poor.

My campaign staff who put the trip together: especially Jacqui Deveneau, Lynne Serpe and Derek Mitchell who, with the help of others, organized everything down to the most minute details.

Blair Bobier, who blogged my journey and stayed in daily contact to make sure I was alright both physically and emotionally.

Maria McMunn, who always says 'yes' and 'I'll help.'

Tracey Grant and Maribeth Stuart, you worked tirelessly keeping the various threads of my home life from unraveling. Tracey, without you I could not have competed this journey; I would have worried too much about my own home.

Loving, *and with all my heart*, thanks to Becky and John – my wonderful children – who don't ever complain about the sacrifices they have made to live with a mom like me.

And in this second edition I would like to thank Chad Bruce. You, dear man, have put your time and talent into creating this new look and correcting errors made in the first edition. Without you, *Left Out in America* would never have become an ebook or had a second run.

And, without Mary Parks, it wouldn't have become this book.

And with the utmost respectful appreciation I thank the homeless people who let me into their lives. It was one of the greatest and saddest gift I have ever been given to hear your stories and live inside our tragic world. I know it is our tragic world, but too many of us never see the reality of it.

In only 14 days I could not possibly have learned more than a fraction of the truth of your lives. Still, I am overwhelmingly grateful to you for showing me the enormity and the intricacy of your personal existences. I walked away from my time with you thinking of the robes worn by the Ghost of Christmas Present in Dickens' *A Christmas Carol*. Under his robes were two children: Want and Ignorance. Remember how they startled Scrooge with their abjectness and their hideousness? "Spirit, are they yours? Scrooge could say no more."

> "'They are Man's,' said the Spirit, looking down upon them. 'And they cling to me, appealing from their fathers. This boy is Ignorance. This girl is Want. Beware them both, and all of their degree, but most of all beware this boy, for on his brow I see that written which is Doom, unless the writing be erased.'"

Thank you for helping to erase some of my ignorance.